Christmas Carol Goes Wrong

Henry Lewis, Jonathan Sayer & Henry Shields

Based on 'A Christmas Carol' by Charles Dickens

methuen | drama

LONDON · NEW YORK · OXFORD · NEW DELHI · SYDNEY

METHUEN DRAMA
Bloomsbury Publishing Plc, 50 Bedford Square, London, WC1B 3DP, UK
Bloomsbury Publishing Inc, 1385 Broadway, New York, NY 10018, USA
Bloomsbury Publishing Ireland, 29 Earlsfort Terrace, Dublin 2, Ireland

BLOOMSBURY, METHUEN DRAMA and the Methuen
Drama logo are trademarks of Bloomsbury Publishing Plc

First published in Great Britain 2025

Copyright © Mischief Worldwide Ltd, 2025

Henry Lewis, Jonathan Sayer and Henry Shields have asserted their right under the
Copyright, Designs and Patents Act, 1988, to be identified as Authors of this work.

Cover Design: Amanda Sutton
Cover Image: Matt Crockett (Dewynters)

All rights reserved. No part of this publication may be: i) reproduced or transmitted in
any form, electronic or mechanical, including photocopying, recording or by means of
any information storage or retrieval system without prior permission in writing from
the publishers; or ii) used or reproduced in any way for the training, development or
operation of artificial intelligence (AI) technologies, including generative AI technologies.
The rights holders expressly reserve this publication from the text and data mining
exception as per Article 4(3) of the Digital Single Market Directive (EU) 2019/790.

Bloomsbury Publishing Plc does not have any control over, or responsibility for,
any third-party websites referred to or in this book. All internet addresses given in this
book were correct at the time of going to press. The authors and publisher regret
any inconvenience caused if addresses have changed or sites have ceased
to exist, but can accept no responsibility for any such changes.

No rights in incidental music or songs contained in the work are hereby granted
and performance rights for any performance/presentation whatsoever
must be obtained from the respective copyright owners.

All rights whatsoever in this play are strictly reserved and application for performance
etc. should be made before rehearsals begin to
United Agents Ltd, 12-26 Lexington Street, London, W1F 0LE.
No performance may be given unless a licence has been obtained.

A catalogue record for this book is available from the British Library.

A catalog record for this book is available from the Library of Congress.

ISBN:	PB:	978-1-3506-1507-6
	ePDF:	978-1-3506-1508-3
	eBook:	978-1-3506-1509-0

Series: Modern Plays

Typeset by Westchester Publishing Services
Printed and bound in Great Britain

To find out more about our authors and books visit
www.bloomsbury.com and sign up for our newsletters.

Christmas Carol Goes Wrong

Henry Lewis, Jonathan Sayer & Henry Shields

Based on 'A Christmas Carol' by Charles Dickens

Kenny Wax and Stage Presence presented the world premiere of the Mischief production *Christmas Carol Goes Wrong* in Salford at the Lowry Theatre on 2 November 2025, followed by a UK tour and West End debut at the Apollo Theatre on 6 December 2025, with the following cast and creative team:

Max	**Matt Cavendish**
Chris	**Daniel Fraser**
Sandra	**Sasha Frost**
Trevor	**Chris Leask**
Robert	**Henry Lewis**
Dennis	**Jonathan Sayer**
Annie	**Dumile Sibanda / Nancy Zamit***
Jonathan	**Greg Tannahill**
Ensemble & Understudies	**Alex Bird, Will Bishop, Siobhan Cha Cha, Colm Gleeson, Ashley Tucker**

Directed by	**Matt DiCarlo**
Set Design	**Libby Todd**
Costume Design	**Roberto Surace**
Lighting Design	**David Howe**
Sound Design & Composition	**Alexandra Faye Braithwaite**

* *The role of Annie was shared.*

Presented by arrangement with Mischief Worldwide Ltd.

MISCHIEF creates award-winning comedy for stage, screen and beyond, with shows continuously playing in the West End for over a decade. Now a global sensation, they are currently bringing joy and laughter to audiences around the world.

Discover more mischief at **mischiefcomedy.com**

Follow us and be social

@mischiefcomedy

FOR MISCHIEF WORLDWIDE LTD

Directors	Mark Bentley, Henry Lewis, Jonathan Sayer, Hilary Strong (Chair), Kenny Wax
CEO	Jo Danvers
Head of Marketing & Brand	Harry Lockyear
Licensing Manager	Jessica Hall
Interim Licensing Manager (Job Share)	Kezia Lockhouse
Marketing Coordinator	Nathan Garwood
Executive Assistant	Dorothy Oehmler
Team Administrator	Jack Cowdery
Consultant Financial Director	Charlotte Johnson
Bookkeeper	Jai Tosniwal
Literary Rights	Nicki Stoddart for United Agents LLP

Christmas Carol Goes Wrong

By Henry Lewis, Jonathan Sayer & Henry Shields

Based on 'A Christmas Carol' by Charles Dickens

Cast

Chris
Robert
Sandra
Dennis
Annie
Max
Jonathan
Trevor

Other roles played by the ensemble.

Settings

Part I

Scene 1 – Auditions
Scene 2 – Production Meeting
Scene 3 – Rehearsals

Part II

Scene 1 – London Street
Scene 2 – Scrooge's Shop
Scene 3 – London Street/Scrooge's Front Door
Scene 4 – Scrooge's Bed Chamber
Scene 5 – School House
Scene 6 – Scrooge's Shop

INTERVAL

Part III

Scene 1 – Scrooge's Bed Chamber
Scene 2 – London Street
Scene 3 – Fred's House
Scene 4 – London Street
Scene 5 – The Cratchit's House
Scene 6 – London Street
Scene 7 – Graveyard of St Barnabus
Scene 8 – Scrooge's Bed Chamber
Scene 9 – London Street/Fred's House

Part IV

Scene 1 – Post Show Drinks

Part I

Scene 1 – AUDITIONS

Music. Spotlight on **Sandra**.

Sandra Marley was dead to begin with. There was no doubt whatever about that. *(Emotional.)* It was Christmas Eve in London town and a chill hung in the air!

Lights up to reveal the empty theatre. **Chris** *and* **Annie** *(in a Christmas jumper) sit behind a desk.*

Chris Stop there. OK, good try.

Annie That was amazing.

Sandra Thanks! I've really been working on my mouth acting.

Chris Mmm. I can see that. Let's try it again but bring it down by ninety-five per cent.

Sandra *(neutral)* Marley was dead to begin with. *(Emotional.)* There was no doubt whatever about that! It was Christmas –

Chris Hold it there!

Annie *applauds.*

Annie So good.

Chris No, that was very emotional now wasn't it?

Sandra I'm an emotional performer. I can do all twelve emotions.

Chris Yes, I can see them on your CV.

Annie Oh, do bafflement!

Sandra *pulls a face.*

Annie Baffling.

Chris I think in this case maybe less is more.

Annie More is more, Chris, that's just maths.

Chris No, less is more.

Sandra So if you want less I should do more?

Chris Yes, but more is less, so I want less, do you understand?

Sandra More or less.

Chris Excellent. Let's try again.

Sandra *takes a big breath in. Silence.*

Sandra (*emotional*) MARLEY WAS DEA –

Chris OK. I think that's more than I need to see.

Sandra Fab. Thanks, Chris.

Annie That was such good acting.

Sandra Oh . . . (*Laughing modestly.*) . . . Yeah, it was. See you at rehearsal!

Annie Merry Christmas! So good!

Sandra *goes.* **Chris** *immediately crumples up her CV and throws it into a waste paper basket.*

Annie She was very watchable.

Chris So's a car crash.

Annie Come on, Chris, you've got to cast someone. Who's gonna be Scrooge?

Chris Well, I'm still considering that role.

Annie (*snorts*) Right.

Chris Trevor. Bring in the next candidate.

Trevor *enters.*

Trevor Right, next up it's Dennis.

Chris Oh God.

Trevor *(reads)* Reading for Bob Cat-shit.

Chris Cratchit.

Trevor Crap-shit.

Trevor *exits*.

Annie Hi, Dennis! How are you?

Dennis Yeah! Really well thanks, I've had a great week and I'm thrilled to be here auditioning for you.

Chris Great, well you're going to be reading for Bob Cratchit.

Dennis Yeah, I think I can.

Chris OK. Do you have any questions before we start?

Dennis Because it's just such a classic Christmas story.

Chris OK, what's going on?

Dennis So many memories.

Annie Dennis. Are you scripting real life conversations again?

Dennis Er ... mainly folk music.

Chris For God's sake.

Annie Dennis, you can't script real life conversations remember. Because the other person won't say what you think they're going to say.

Dennis Winter, definitely.

Chris DENNIS!

Dennis *snaps out of his script*.

Dennis Sorry, I'm just a bit nervous.

Annie Don't be nervous. It's only me and Chris.

Dennis I just …um … I really want this hang out to go well.

Chris Well, this isn't a hang out, this is an audition.

Dennis But can I count it though … in my friendship journal?

Annie Yeah, course you can.

Chris What? No! This is an audition. It has nothing to do with friendship. Do not mark this down as friendship in any document. That's fraud. Do you want to go to jail?

Dennis Well, it would be friendship if after the audition we went for a drink at the Dead Duck. I brought money.

Chris Let's just do the scene.

Dennis Annie?

Pause.

Annie I really want to say yes, but my mouth won't do the shape.

So … Bob Cratchit.

Dennis Oh, I wanted to try Fred.

Chris Why?

Dennis He's just really fun and popular.

Chris But you're miserable and annoying, which is why you'd be perfect for Cratchit.

Dennis But I've learnt the Fred lines.

Chris I sincerely doubt that.

Dennis And I've been watching other people who have friends from a distance for years.

Annie Come on, Chris, give him a chance.

Chris Alright, come on then. Do a bit of your Fred.

Dennis (*as Fred*) Christmas, though it has never put a scrap of gold in my pocket –

Chris That's enough thanks.

Dennis Do you want to see any more?

Chris I've seen all I need to see. Don't call us.

Dennis You'll call me?

Chris No.

Dennis Drink at the Dead Duck?

Chris *closes the door, crumples the CV and throws it away.*

Annie Why don't you give him a go as Fred. He really wants to do it.

Chris He's not likeable. Why don't you play Fred. Everyone seems to like you. Your lack of intelligence puts them at ease. Trevor, who's next?

Trevor *comes, not looking up from his clipboard.*

Trevor Robert's here.

Robert Enter stage right.

Annie Hi, Robert. How are you?

Robert Very well. Thanks so much for coming in.

Robert *pulls up a chair and takes out some papers.*

Chris Thank you for coming in.

Robert My pleasure. Right. In your own time.

Chris What?! What are you doing?

Robert I'm auditioning you.

Chris I'm the director. Why would an actor be auditioning a director?

Robert To make sure we don't get a bad one like we had on Snow White.

Chris I directed Snow White.

Robert Exactly.

Chris No, Robert I am here to audition you.

Robert Fine. I'll 'audition' then. To be or not to be!

Chris No, we're doing *A Christmas Carol*.

Robert Good to know, I'll be Scrooge. Here's my CV.

Robert drops a massive folder onto the desk and then brings out a small acting trophy and places it on top.

Chris Let's do Act 1, Scene 2.

Robert Fine.

Chris When you're ready.

Robert Right. What are the lines?

Chris You haven't learnt it.

Robert I haven't read it.

Chris This is a waste of time.

Robert It's fine, I can improvise. Here we go. 'Run Mary, there's a troll in the woods.'

Chris Wait. That's not in *A Christmas Carol*.

Annie But that was great, Chris, we should put that in.

Chris No!

Robert Alright, I'll try something else. 'I'm Santa, grab your hatchet, we must rescue Mary' –

Chris No. There is no Mary!

Annie I'll be Mary! Quick Santa, pass me that grenade. The man-eating troll is coming!

Robert We'll blast him with our laser vision!

Robert	**Annie**
(*firing pretend laser*)	(*firing pretend laser*)
Bebebebebebebee!	Bebebebebebebee!

Chris No! No! None of this is in *A Christmas Carol*!

Robert Alright, you show us how it's done.

Chris Fine, I will, I will!

Chris *gets up and comes into the space.* **Robert** *sits in* **Chris***'s seat.*

Bah humbug. What is Christmas but a time to find yourself a year older but not an hour richer.

Robert Hmm, it's not quite working, but thanks for coming in.

Chris Ah, well thanks for seeing me – no, wait! Get out, you are not auditioning me!

Robert *crumples* **Chris***'s CV and throws it in the bin.*

Chris Annie! Robert, I am not letting you play Scrooge and I am not letting you take over, now get out!

Annie He's good though! He's got more gravitas than you've got neck tension.

Robert Look, can I have one more chance at Scrooge?

Chris Absolutely not.

Robert Please, Chris.

Chris Robert, Scrooge is a real role with depth and nuance. Your natural casting is as one of the Ugly Sisters in a third-rate panto. Goodbye. Trevor!

Trevor *opens the door.* **Robert** *exits.*

Trevor Next up Jonathan. He wants to play (*Reads.*) The Christmas Ghost who's about to come.

Jonathan *enters.*

Jonathan It's the Ghost of Christmas Yet to Come.

Trevor Urgh, poor guy.

Annie Jonathan! I thought you'd quit acting?

Jonathan Well yeah, my therapist said I had some residual trauma from Peter Pan so I should stop performing, but then Chris called and said I had to get back on the horse, even if the horse is wild and might kill you. So here I am. But baby steps, I don't want any lines.

Chris No, you can actually act. We can't waste you on a non-speaking role. I was thinking of you for the Ghost of Jacob Marley. Big entrance, you'd fly in.

Jonathan But my therapist was very clear that I shouldn't fly again.

Chris OK, well let's just see how we go.

Jonathan I can't go upstairs any more.

Chris That's fine.

Jonathan I've moved into a bungalow.

Chris OK, well we'll cross that bridge when we come to it.

Jonathan I can't cross bridges.

Chris Look, you're not going to be high. Just give it a go. Stand on the chair.

Jonathan I don't think I should.

Chris Just one foot.

Vamp as they go back and forth. **Jonathan** *finally puts a foot on the chair.*

Jonathan No, I'm not sure.

Chris There we go, one more foot.

Jonathan *puts his second foot on the chair. He immediately has a traumatic flashback and starts weeping.*

Jonathan ARGHHH! No! NO!

Chris OK, just step off.

Jonathan Let me down! LET ME DOWN!

Annie *and* **Chris** *help* **Jonathan** *down.*

Jonathan I WANT TO GROW UP! I'M A MAN, NOT A BOY!

Chris Alright, thank you, Jonathan. Trevor!

Trevor *enters.*

Trevor What have you done to him?

Chris Take him outside.

Trevor *takes* **Jonathan** *outside. Silence.*

Chris Why do the talented ones always snap?

Chris *crumples the CV and throws it in the bin.*

Trevor Alright, next up we've got a new one.

Chris Ah, some new blood. Send him in.

Trevor This is . . . *(Reads.)* Burt.

Robert *enters (in glasses and a fake moustache).*

Robert *(thinly disguised voice)* Hello, I am Burt, auditioning for Scrooge.

Chris Robert.

Robert I have prepared a song. *(Sings.)* 'Look out, Mary, The trolls are scary!'

Chris ROBERT! GET OUT!

Robert   Fine.

Robert *slopes to the door.*

Trevor   Told you it wouldn't work, mate.

Robert   Shut up, Trevor.

Robert *exits.*

Trevor   This is Max. Reading for *(Reads from a clipboard.)* Young Scrog-ee.

Max *enters holding a plastic bag.* **Trevor** *exits.*

Annie   Hi, Max!

Max *(smiling)*   Hi. Nice jumper!

Annie   Oh thanks!

Max   Sorry I'm late, I was getting Sandra's Christmas present. Took me a while but I smashed it.

Annie   What did you get her?

Max   A mirror. Bit of a shame really.

He jingles the bag of mirror shards.

Chris   Fine, let's look at Act One, Scene Six. Annie will read in for Belle.

Annie *(reads)*   I'm sorry, Ebenezer, we cannot be together any longer.

Max/Young Scrooge *(smiling)*   But Belle, my heart is broken.

Chris   Right, stop there.

Annie   Amazing.

Chris   No. Why are you laughing?

Max *(laughing)*   I wasn't.

Chris   Yes you were. It's a sad scene. Belle, who you love, is leaving you. Let's try again. Annie.

Annie *(reads)*   I'm sorry, Ebenezer. We cannot be together any longer.

Max/Young Scrooge *(laughing)*   But Belle, my heart is broken.

Chris   Stop. No. You're still smiling.

Max *(laughing)*   Was I?

Chris   Yeah. You're still smiling now.

Max *(laughing)*   Am I?

Chris   Yes.

Max   How about now?

Still smiling.

Chris   Yes.

Max *(looking down seriously)*   OK, hold on, hold on, I can get this, hold on, hold on, hold on.

Max *looks up, smiling immediately.*

Chris   STOP SMILING!

Max *(laughing)*   Sorry, I'm a bit off my game this morning. I nearly got hit by a big, yellow transit can.

Max *laughs. He mimes dodging the van.*

Map   Oop! *(Suddenly screams.)* AAAAAAAAH!!! *(Goes back to laughing.)*

Silence.

Chris   Thank you, Max.

Max   Do I get the part?

Chris   We'll let you know.

Chris *crumples his CV and throws it in the bin.*

Max   Merry Christmas.

Chris *slams the door in his face.*

Annie I really liked him. He's got such a positive energy.

Chris He's too positive for Cornley. It's like Tinky-Winky turning up in a Tarantino film.

Annie He liked my jumper.

Chris You shouldn't be wearing that, Christmas isn't for another three weeks.

Annie I have to, it's freezing. Can we put the heater on?

Chris No. That thing costs a fortune. Trevor, who's next.

Trevor Next up. Clint Beef.

Clint *enters. It's* **Robert** *in a much more elaborate disguise.*

Clint Hello, I'm Clint Beef!

Chris No, Robert!

Robert Fine. Look, who's going to play Scrooge? I think it's clear I'm the best option. MARY!

Chris No! I just. I have to think about it.

Annie (*smirks*) Classic.

Chris Excuse me?

Annie You do this every time.

Chris Do what?

Annie You always start auditions saying anyone could play the lead, but in the end you always cast yourself.

Robert That's why his old drama group kicked him out.

Chris That's not . . . They didn't kick me out and I don't always play the lead.

Annie Alright, well who are you going cast as Scrooge then?

Chris Well . . . I – I – I . . . haven't considered it yet.

Annie Who's it gonna be, Chris?

Chris Well, I just . . . I ... I ... I ... need a bit more time to –

Annie Who are you going to cast as Scrooge?!

Chris Robert. I cast Robert.

Robert Yes! Thank you, Chris! We will be going with a different director though.

Chris Robert! See, I'm not this control freak you're painting me as. I'm very happy with Robert as the lead. Now we have to cast these other roles. Who's next?

Annie That's everyone.

Chris There's no one else?

Annie You've seen the best and brightest Cornley has to offer.

Robert Inbreeding has devastated this village.

Chris How many people have we auditioned?

Annie Five.

Chris And how many roles are there in *A Christmas Carol*?

Annie Thirty-three.

Chris Then what was the point in even doing auditions?

Annie *pours the bin out onto the table.*

Annie Well, we have our cast.

Scene 2 – PRODUCTION MEETING

A sign reading PRODUCTION MEETING now hangs on the wall. **Annie, Robert, Chris, Trevor** *and* **Sandra** *sit at a large table. All in Christmas jumpers.*

Annie (*reads*)   Page 18. Minutes from previous production meeting continued.

7:47 Sandra said 'Is it really essential to read the minutes from the previous production meeting, it takes so long to get through them'. 7:48 Chris replied: 'It is essential to have the minutes read in full to ensure everyone is up to speed on what happened at the last production meeting in case anyone was absent from that production meeting'. Sandra asked: 'Was anyone absent from the last production meeting?' I consulted the minutes from the last production meeting and confirmed that everyone in attendance had also been in attendance at the last production meeting. 7:49 Robert stood up and said: 'What a load of bollocks. What a colossal load of mind-numbing bollocks. Why, if we were all here at the last production meeting do we need to re-read the minutes from that production meeting, we were all bloody there, weren't we?' I minuted that.

Sandra said: 'Will you please stop minuting. This is insane, we're only going to have to listen to all this read back again next week.'

7:50 I replied: 'I'm only doing what I've been asked to do.'

Sandra said: 'We could all be in the pub right now.'

Robert said: 'I wouldn't go to the Dead Duck, the landlord's livid since someone nicked his pub sign. Annie, you're not minuting all this are you?' I confirmed I was minuting all this.

Robert said: 'Just take the pen away from her. For God's sake take the pen away! If we take her pen we take her power.'

7:51 Sandra snatched the pen from my ha –

(Pause.)

Chris Thank you, Annie. Now how many minutes do we have left of this meeting?

Annie Nine.

Chris And how many items on the agenda?

Robert Nine.

Chris God, OK. One minute per item. That's fine. We'll just have to be efficient.

Robert Authority taken!

Robert *grabs a stopwatch and starts it.*

I will hold us to exact timing. First item lighting. Go.

Chris OK, well we don't need exact timings.

Robert Fifty-nine! Fifty-eight!

Chris Trevor, tell us about the lighting design.

Trevor We've got six lights up in the rig.

A lamp falls from the rig.

Trevor We've got five lights up in the rig.

Chris Why are they falling down?

Trevor It's all part of the process. The unsafe ones fall. It's natural selection.

Chris I thought Trevor's brother was getting safety chains?

Annie He got hit by that yellow transit van.

Sandra God, another one! I read about that in the Cornley Gazette, no one knows who the driver is.

Chris Falling lights are extremely dangerous.

Trevor No, that's not the dangerous thing. The dangerous thing that we all have to talk about is –

Robert Time. Moving on, next item.

Chris OK, but we need to hear what the dangerous thing is.

Robert Move on, Chris, fifty-six seconds left on opening night guest list.

Annie I'm trying to get celebrity guests, I've sent an invite to Charles Dickens but I haven't heard back yet.

Chris Annie –

Annie All these stuck-up authors never get back to us. We had the same thing with Oscar Wilde last year.

And when we did Noah's Ark, I didn't hear back from Matthew, Mark, Luke or John. You'd think one would drop me an email.

Trevor Their loss, mate. Noah's Ark was bangin'.

Sandra Yeah, only having badgers turned out to be a real blessing in disguise.

Robert (*sings*) *The badgers came in two by two*

Hurrah –

All (*joining in*) *– hurrah.*

More badgers came in two by two

Hurrah, hurrah.

More badgers came in two by two

More badgers and other badgers too

And they all came into the ark

There's too many badgers in here.

Vamp as cast congratulate themselves etc.

Robert Time. Moving on. Next item. Choreography. Go!

Chris Well, this is a play, there is no choreography.

Robert Fine, then we'll just wait.

Pause.

Chris Well, this is a waste of time, let's move on to set design.

Robert No. Please, Chris. This minute is allocated specifically to discuss choreography.

Silence. **Chris** *becoming frustrated.*

Annie Can we go back –

Robert No. Forty more seconds on choreography.

Pause.

Chris Robert, this is –

Robert Ba! Ba! Ba!

Silence.

Twenty more seconds.

Chris Robert –

Robert Chris, you wanted us to keep to time.

Chris But there is no choreography.

Robert Then there will be silence.

Silence.

Ten.

Silence.

Sandra Wait a minute, isn't there a dance in the Fezziwig Ball?

Annie Oh yeah!

Robert Time. Next item.

Annie But the dance!

Robert We'll just have to do knee bends or something.

Chris But we were just getting onto –

Robert NEXT ITEM, CHRIS! WALK AWAY! WALK AWAY NOW!

Chris Right, give me the stopwatch. Your authority is rescinded.

Robert You will rue this day, Chris Bean.

Chris Moving on to set design …

All the others ooh and aah in anticipation. **Chris** *moves covered model box into the centre.*

Right, it's very delicate. No one touch anything.

Chris *whips the cloth off and everyone immediately reaches in to touch everything.*

Chris NO! NO!

Chris *takes the items back from everyone's hands.*

Chris That's the office, that's the bedroom. And after the interval there's -

Annie Ooh, what happens in the interval?

Chris Well the curtain comes in

Sandra Ooh, what does the curtain look like?

Chris It's just a curtain. But Act 2 starts with –

Trevor I can't visualise this curtain...

Chris It's just a curtain! Annie, get some scrap paper.

Annie I'll use Robert's CV.

Annie *hands* **Robert**'s *CV to* **Chris**, *who holds* **Robert**'s *CV in place as a curtain.*

Trevor Ah, a curtain!

Chris Then Act 2 – *We hear a sudden hammering on the dock doors.*

Chris Oh that's mother dropping off Tiny Tim. No one touch the model box.

Chris *exits.*

Robert Come on, there can't be any harm in touching one –

Robert *reaches in.*

Robert Oh, no, that has broken immediately.

Sandra Robert! You've bent the lamppost!

Sandra *reaches in to fix it.*

Robert No! You've torn the storeroom door off!

Sandra Oh no!

Robert Here, use the Maltesers for the storeroom door.

Sandra You can't use Maltesers!

Robert It looks fine. Chris won't notice.

Another lamp falls from the rig, crushing the model box.

Robert He might notice that.

Sandra Trevor!

Trevor Only when the weak have fallen, will the lighting rig be strong.

Sandra Fred's House is completely crushed.

Annie Here use this, I got my niece a Kelly's Dreamhouse for Christmas. We can borrow the kitchen, just be careful not to tear the –

Trevor *tears open the box and puts the kitchen in.*

24 Christmas Carol Goes Wrong

Trevor Got it!

Annie Trev!

Kelly V/O Let's bake cookies!

Chris *enters, unseen, with a bag.*

Trevor Do you think Chris'll notice?

Chris Notice what?

Trevor Err ... Sandra's Christmas jumper.

Sandra It's new!

Chris I don't know why you all insist on wearing those. Christmas is still eight days away.

Trevor *covers the model box and wheels it away.*

Chris Where are you taking the model box?

Trevor Just getting it ready to go off to the builders.

Chris Well, make sure it gets there safely.

Trevor Yeah, no worries, I'll whack it in me transit van.

Chris Now, moving on to casting. Everyone meet Tiny Tim!

Chris *takes out a disturbing looking ventriloquist's dummy in a tuxedo. Everyone is spooked 'argh' etc.*

Robert Chris, we can't use that.

Sandra We're supposed to want Tiny Tim to live.

Chris What's the matter with you all? I've had Mr Garibaldi ever since I was a little boy.

Trevor That makes so much sense.

Robert Chris, you should throw that away.

Chris Mother tried a few times but he always seemed to just . . . come back.

Sandra I'm not doing any scenes with that.

Chris Oh come on, he's cute! Hello!

Sandra *throws* **Mr Garibaldi** *to* **Trevor** *who puts* **Mr Garibaldi** *into the model box and closes the lid.*

Chris You can put him in a box, Trevor, but when you wake up he'll be back in your bed.

Annie So we've got Tiny Tim.

Sandra And the Cornley Youth Theatre are playing all the ensemble roles.

Chris Are they ready?

Sandra I've taught them all twelve emotions, and they're into module three of mouth acting. OOOOOOH!

Robert OOOOOOH!

Sandra Sorry Robert, you're just not getting it.

Robert Damn! It's just embarrassing. I'm the only one in the class older than nine.

Chris Trevor, are you still OK to play the Ghost of Christmas Yet to Come?

Trevor Yeah, I've actually been thinking a lot about me character.

Chris Right, well remember the Ghost of Christmas Yet to Come is just a silent, hooded figure.

Trevor I wanna play him Scottish?

Chris What? Why?

Trevor Wanna show me range, played Peter Pan, did him scouse, played Florence Colleymoore, did her scouse. Played Paul McCartney, did him French. Now I wanna try Scottish.

Chris Right, but he doesn't have any lines and he's cloaked from head to toe.

Trevor Yeah. Yeah. Yeah.

Chris But you want to play him Scottish?

Trevor Yeah. Yeah. Yeah.

Chris Even though we'll never see or hear him?

Trevor Yeah. Yeah. Yeah.

Chris Alright, he's Scottish. Right, how much is left on the agenda?

Annie Five items.

Chris And how long left of the meeting?

Robert Eleven seconds.

Chris Oh my God.

Robert Rue! RUE!

Chris Next item!

Trevor Sound.

Chris We'll need it.

Annie Props.

Chris Ebay.

Sandra Marketing.

Chris Posters.

Annie Sales.

Chris None.

Trevor The afterparty.

Chris Absolutely not!

Robert That's time! Meeting adjourned.

Everyone starts to pack up.

Sandra Wait, what about press?

Robert We didn't get there, LEAVE IT, Sandra.

Sandra So I guess you don't want to know about the reviewer?

All stop.

Chris What?

Annie A reviewer?

Pause.

Robert Meeting unadjourned.

Sandra Listen, we all know the *Cornley Gazette*'s official policy has been not to review our shows since our immersive production of Dracula.

Robert The small print on the ticket clearly said I would enter his house and bite him.

Sandra Well, their critic Brian Bentley says he's going to come and review Christmas Carol!

They react with amazement.

Sandra I might get a mention! One good mention could lead to an interview, an interview could lead to an agent, an agent could lead to an audition, an audition could lead to Hollywood and me playing Russell Crowe's dead wife in a flashback!

Chris Robert.

Chris *and* **Robert** *step aside.*

Chris If there's a reviewer in we need our best actor in the lead role.

Robert Absolutely. I won't let you down.

Chris No, you are not our best actor. You are a gibbon in a man suit. I'll be playing Scrooge.

Robert Oh come on!

Chris I'm sorry. My decision is final.

Robert Chris, your behaviour is unacceptable.

Chris My behaviour?

Robert Yes. Belittling everyone, refusing to heat the building, and now you're reneging on casting decisions.

Annie Yeah, we all just want to get into the Christmas spirit and you're ruining it.

Chris Christmas spirit is not a real thing. It's a marketing tool used to sell Coca-Cola. I don't care about you or your precious little feelings. I care about getting a good review and about my production being a success. So you will all shut up and do as you're told. Meeting re-adjourned.

He takes a sweet from the table.

Chris Ah, humbug.

Scene 3 – REHEARSALS

Full company are rehearsing with **Chris** *dressed in a Scrooge gown. Everyone else in Christmas jumpers.*

Chris Bah humbug.

Dennis *mimes entering.*

Dennis/Cratchit Merry . . . um –

Chris Christmas! Obviously Christmas, isn't it?

Dennis/Cratchit Merry Christmas, Mr . . . Mr –

Chris Mr Scrooge! It's Scrooge, isn't it!

Dennis Oh sorry.

Chris Dennis, we're so behind. You don't know any lines at all? It's not good enough! This is our last rehearsal. We open at the weekend.

Dennis I wanted to play Fred! I learnt Fred! It took me months! Now I have to learn Cratchit *in* – *(Counts on his hand.)* Wednesday, Thursday, Friday. Two days!

Max Oh, I love rehearsals. The dusty theatre floor, the sound of the director screaming at people, the taste of the greasepaint.

Sandra Max, have you been eating the greasepaint again?

Max *(chuckling)*   Yeah . . .

Dennis Does anyone want to grab a drink later? Sandra?

Sandra Uh ... Butternut squash!

Max Oh. Sandra, could you help me with something?

Sandra Yep.

Jonathan Chris, the window in Scrooge's bedroom has arrived and it looks very high.

Chris Let's please just rehearse. Bah humbug!

Annie Chris, we need to talk props.

Chris Not now, Annie.

Annie This can't wait! I'm locked in a bidding war for a Victorian candlestick!

Robert Go all in!

Annie *(typing on her phone)*   Eight hundred pounds!

Chris No, Robert. Annie, do not spend eight hundred pounds.

Annie And someone needs to sort the bags of snow.

Dennis I'll do it, I can help!

Chris You can't be trusted.

Dennis I can! I just got a promotion at work. Now I'm in charge of the pens. Oh! I left the pens on the bus.

Chris No, Dennis.

Dennis Please Chris, I will prove that I'm friendship material.

Dennis *goes to get the bags of snow.*

Sandra *(on phone)* No, no, no, no!

She hangs up.

AAAH! How could they do this to me?!

Max What's happened?

Sandra The Cornley Youth Theatre have pulled out! The parents don't want the children taking part, cause one of the kids had a massive tantrum.

Robert Bethany stole my apple slices. There are consequences to actions!

Christ Sandra, you promised me an ensemble! Figure it out!

Sandra *is distraught.*

Max Don't worry, I'll do it.

Sandra All sixteen parts?

Max *(laughs)* Yeah.

Sandra Thanks, Max.

Robert Things would be going much smoother if I was playing Scrooge.

Chris Robert, we have been over this! The Ghost of Christmas Present is a good role.

Robert But he doesn't even come on until the second half! Our audience is normally long gone by then.

Chris You can be in the first scene, you can be the clerk.

Robert Does the clerk even have any lines?

Sandra (*looking at the script*) Yes.

Robert What are they?

Sandra That's it, just 'yes' on page three.

Robert Chris!

Chris My decision is final. Bah humbug!

Annie (*on phone*) Chris, it's the builders! They want to know if you want the set built exactly like the model box?

Chris Of course, that's the whole point of the model box!

Jonathan *approaches* **Chris** *with a pair of ordinary shoes.*

Jonathan Chris, I can't wear these shoes, they're too high!

Chris NO MORE INTERRUPTIONS!

Annie Chris, stop shouting, you're upsetting Dennis.

Max Yeah, he looks distraught.

Dennis No, that's just my face.

Sandra That's why when we did Snow White we had to change Happy to Traumatized.

Dennis *approaches with two big bags.*

Dennis Chris, I've got the fake snow and the plastic coins.

Chris Put the snow up in the rig, put the coins on the desk. Can you do that?

Dennis I will give it my very best attempt.

Annie Chris, I need you to authorise a bigger spend on the candlestick! We're going to lose it!

Jonathan Chris, I've just got the sheet music for the Fezziwig song. I can't sing this. It's too high.

Robert Chris, we need to talk.

Chris I've made my decision, Robert.

Robert But please, Chris. My son's coming to see this.

Chris What's your son got to do with it?

Robert Fleance has to have a good time. He never comes to our shows, he's always too busy with his step-dad.

Chris Robert, there are certain things in life that are never going to happen. Sandra's never going to be in a Russell Crowe movie. Dennis is never going to make any friends and you will never get to play Scrooge unless I'm completely incapacitated.

Robert Really.

Chris Now, just please let me rehearse!

Dennis *mimes entering.*

Dennis/Cratchit Merry Scrooge, Mr Christmas!

Chris Bah humbug. Christmas is a ti –

Annie *starts to open the noisy electric dock door.* **Chris** *tries to keep rehearsing underneath.*

Robert (*to* **Annie**) What are you doing?

Annie (*to* **Robert**) Trevor just text, he's bringing the van round with the gravestones.

Vamp as **Jonathan** *and* **Max** *start singing,* **Robert** *and* **Annie** *argue about the door whilst* **Chris** *tries to continue rehearsing.*

Chris (*trying to speak over the dock door*) Bah humbug. Christmas is a . . . Christmas is a day not a year older than . . . No, Christmas is a time for every man who goes around with Christmas, no, any man who . . . WILL YOU SHUT UP! JUST SHUT UP.

Annie *stops opening the door.*

Chris   I'M TRYING TO REHEARSE MY MONOLOGUE. WE HAVE NO MORE REHEARSALS AFTER THIS SO NO MORE INTERRUPTIONS!

The front of a yellow transit van bursts the through the wall on the opposite side of the stage to the dock door. **Trevor** *dressed in a big black raincoat with the hood up, carrying a gravestone under his arm gets out of the van and enters through the dock door.*

Trevor *(putting his hood down)*   Alright everyone! I've got the gravestones. What happened to the wall?

Chris   Trevor, you idiot!

Trevor   Oi! Where's the gratitude? I'm working hard for you! I've just won a vicious bidding war for a Victorian candlestick.

Chris   Can you not do anything right?!

Trevor   I've got the gravestone bang on. Look.

He puts the gravestone down and points at it. It reads CHRIS BEAN.

Chris   That's my name!

Trevor   Yeah, is that not what you wanted?

Chris   WHY WOULD I WANT MY OWN – You are all <u>morons</u>! None of you are capable of anything.

Dennis   Four days! Sorry I miscounted.

Chris   ARGHHHHH!

Trevor   Oi, cool your boots, Chrissy. You can't speak to people like that. I'm warning you if you keep on like this, you'll end up alone and miserable with no friends, no drama society, and no one who cares about you.

Sandra He's right, Chris. At this rate you're going to be less popular than Dennis.

Dennis To walk a mile in my shoes is to walk alone.

Chris I don't care! You are not my friends. I don't want to be your friend. You all disgust me!!! I hate the sight of all of you. You're ruining my production, you're ruining my Christmas and you've ruined my life. After Saturday I hope I never have to see any of you again! Merry Christmas!

Blackout. Merry Christmas bells. We transition to opening night. **Chris** *enters stage left and takes his place in the spotlight centre stage. Show cloth flies in.*

Merry Christmas! Good evening and welcome to Cornley Drama Society's production of *A Christmas Carol*. Please do not report this performance to the local council. We have had a wonderful rehearsal process, it's been a really festive treat. I am Chris Bean the director, and I'd like to say a huge thank you to Chris Bean the actor who had to valiantly step in at the last minute to take on the role of Scrooge. I'm welcome. Apologies to anyone feeling a little chilly in the auditorium, unfortunately a yellow transit punctured a hole through the back wall of the theatre days ago. We called the local council to have the van removed but the surveyor told us that the bonnet and front axle are now structurally integral to the building. On top of that, we do prefer to keep the heating off for budgetary reasons. And of course, a number of our previous shows have been inadvertently sabotaged by the heat. I'm of course referring to our production of Disney's classic *Defrosted*, the heartwarming Raymond Briggs classic *The Snowman*, which we had to rename *The Carrot in The Puddle*, and of course last year's seasonal spectacular *Cinderella on Water*. Now the stage is set, the actors are prepared, please sit back and enjoy Charles Dickens ... es *A Christmas Carol*.

Part II

PERFORMANCE

Scene 1 – LONDON STREET

Lights up to reveal a Victorian street. Stage right is the exterior of Scrooge's shop, which reads SCROOGE AND MARLEY – EST. 1815. A hanging pub sign reads DEAD DUCK. A spotlight comes up on **Sandra** *(as* **Narrator***).*

Sandra/Narrator Marley was dead to begin with. There was no doubt whatever about that. It was Christmas Eve in London town a chill hung in the air. The city clocks had only just gone three, but it was quite dark already–it had not been light all day–and candles were flaring in the windows of the neighbouring offices. The fog came pouring in every keyhole. Even though every street was narrow, the houses opposite were mere phantoms. All the goodly folk hurried back and forth with smiles upon their faces and joy in their hearts. All except one. The tall, twisted figure of Ebenezer Scrooge cut quickly through the crowd.

Chris *enters (as* **Scrooge***) and walks downstage.*

Sandra/Narrator Scrooge was a tight-fisted hand at the grindstone

A light falls from the rig. **Trevor** *walks onstage and picks it up.*

Sandra/Narrator A squeezing, wrenching, grasping, scraping, clutching, covetous old sinner.

Chris *walks off behind the shop.*

Scene 2 – SCROOGE'S SHOP

A gloomy office with a partner's desks, door to the street, a double window (covered by a blind). Shelves of books line the walls and a chandelier hangs from the centre of the room. A rolling ladder stands

against one of the shelf stacks. Stage right is a wall-sized box of Maltesers that has replaced flattage and door to an off stage storeroom. **Dennis** (*as* **Bob Cratchit**) *is reading lines from papers at a desk and* **Robert** (*as a* **Clerk** *with a cane*) *is working at the back.*

Sandra/Narrator External cold had little influence on Scrooge, no warmth could warm him, no wintery weather chill him.

Chris *enters from the back, the low door knocking off his top hat.*

Sandra/Narrator No wind that blew was bitterer than he.

Sandra *exits.*

Dennis/Cratchit Merry Christmas, Mr Scrooge!

Chris/Scrooge Bah humbug. What is Christmas but a time to find yourself a year older but not an hour richer?

Dennis/Cratchit (*he forgets his line and reads from a book*) Oh Mr Scrooge. Christmas is no time to think of money. Next line in desk. (*Opens desk.*) Look at my happy smiling face. It is there because I think of those I love. (*Lowers the desk, not smiling.*)

Chris/Scrooge It is a wise time to think of money when others think of nought but how to take it from you. Clerk.

Robert *seethes.*

Chris/Scrooge I want a list of every tenant behind on their payments. Can you have it drawn up by the end of the day?

Robert/Clerk Yes.

Robert *gets to work.*

Dennis/Cratchit (*reading*) But it's Christmas Eve, sir. You have no lines for a while now. Stay where you are and do not wander off.

Chris/Scrooge And now, time to sit in peace and count the day's takings.

Robert (*improvises*) Allow me, sir.

Chris/Scrooge (*improvises*)   Thank you, CLERRRK!

Robert *helps* **Chris** *into his chair but pulls it out from under him and* **Chris** *falls out of sight behind the desk.*

Robert   Time to sit in peace and count the da –

Chris *gets back to his feet.*

Chris   Robert!

Robert   Humbug!

Chris/Scrooge   Thank you, Clerk!

Robert *slinks into the background.* **Annie** *enters (as* **Fred***).*

Annie/Fred   Merry Christmas, Uncle, God save you.

Chris/Scrooge   Here comes another festive fool. What right have you to be merry? You're poor enough.

Annie/Fred   What right have you to be dismal? You're rich enough. And good tidings to you, Bob.

Annie *opens her coat revealing* **Dennis***'s next line underneath.*

Dennis/Cratchit (*reads*)   Merry Christmas, Mr Fred.

Annie/Fred   I hope Tiny Tim is well.

Annie *takes off her jacket to reveal* **Dennis***'s next line.*

Dennis/Cratchit (*reads*)   He grows stronger every day!

Annie/Fred   He takes after his father, does he not?

Annie *takes off her top hat to reveal an Alice band with a piece of paper stuck to it reading HA HA HA.*

Dennis/Cratchit (*reads*)   Ha. Ha. Ha.

Annie *replaces her hat.*

Dennis/Cratchit (*reads from jacket*)   Hang jacket.

Dennis *drops* **Annie***'s jacket and takes his own off, hanging it by the door.*

Chris/Scrooge Every idiot who goes about with Merry Christmas on his lips should be boiled with his own pudding and buried with a stake of holly through his heart.

Annie/Fred Christmas, though it has never put a scrap of gold in my pocket has done me good and will do me good and I say God bless it! Now, let us toast. Have you any brandy?

Chris/Scrooge Drink my brandy, will you? Another fine way to pick a man's pocket.

Annie/Fred Please, Uncle!

Chris/Scrooge If it will hasten your departure so be it. Clerk, find the bottle in the storeroom that old Fezziwig left behind.

Robert *turns stage right and opens the perforated flap of the Maltesers spilling football-sized Maltesers onto the stage.* **Robert** *pushes them all back inside the box and closes himself in.*

Annie/Fred Bob, you must share a glass too. Although only one! It's still a working day.

Annie *lifts up her hat to reveal the Alice band again.*

Dennis/Cratchit (*reads*) Ha! Ha! Ha!

All *drink except* **Robert***, who leaves his glass on a shelf. The bell over the door rings as* **Sandra** *(as* **Charity Collector***) enters.*

Chris/Scrooge Who is it now?

Sandra/Collector Have I the pleasure of addressing Mr Scrooge or Mr Marley?

Chris/Scrooge Mr Marley died seven years ago this very day. I am Mr Scrooge, what is it you want?

Sandra/Collector We're raising money for the needy in the poorhouse, sir. More are lost to the cold at Christmas than any other week of the year.

Annie/Fred God rest their souls.

Annie *and* **Dennis** *both take off their hats.* **Dennis** *sees the headband again.*

Dennis/Cratchit   Ha. Ha. Ha.

Annie *quickly replaces the hat.*

Chris/Scrooge   Are there no prisons?

Sandra/Collector   Plenty of prisons.

Chris/Scrooge   Oh! I was afraid that something had occurred to stop them in their useful course. I'm very glad to hear it.

Sandra/Collector   What may I put you down for, sir?

Chris/Scrooge   Nothing.

Sandra/Collector   You wish to be anonymous?

Chris/Scrooge   I wish to be left alone.

Sandra/Collector   But what would you want for the needy?

Chris *crosses the room.*

Chris/Scrooge   That they should die and decrease the surplus population.

Sandra/Collector   I see.

Dennis/Cratchit (*reading from bag*)   I have not much in my coin purse.

Dennis *takes a smaller purse out of the bag.*

Dennis/Cratchit (*reads*)   But what little I have you are welcome to.

Dennis *takes out an even smaller coin purse.*

Dennis/Cratchit (*reads*)   There is only a single penny I have saved.

Sandra/Collector   You'd part with your only coin?

Dennis *takes a penny out of the coin purse and reads off of it.*

Dennis/Cratchit (*reads*)   Yes.

Sandra/Collector   Do you not need it for your family?

Dennis *turns the coin and reads off the back.*

Dennis/Cratchit (*reads*)   No.

Sandra/Collector   Thank you, Mr Cratchit, you'd give all you have to charity?

Dennis/Cratchit (*reads*)   No.

Sandra/Collector   No? You don't want to give to charity?

Dennis/Cratchit (*reads*)   Yes?

Sandra/Collector   Are you sure?

Dennis/Cratchit   No.

Chris/Scrooge   Make a choice. You have to make a choice. Will you give them the coin?

Dennis *flips the coin and reads.*

Dennis/Cratchit (*reads*)   Yes.

Sandra *grabs the coin.*

Sandra/Collector   Thank you.

Dennis *reads off his bag.*

Dennis/Cratchit   Made in China.

Annie/Fred   Uncle! If Bob can afford to part with a penny when he has so little, surely you can part with a farthing.

Chris/Scrooge   So be it. One farthing it is. As long as this means all of you will leave me in peace.

Chris *upends a money bag onto the desk, lots of snow pours out. He grabs a handful of snow and hands it to* **Sandra**.

Chris/Scrooge   There we are. One farthing.

Sandra/Collector   Thank you, Mr Scrooge. Merry Christmas!

Annie *picks up a Malteaser.*

Annie/Fred   Here. Take a big Malteaser for the poor.

Sandra/Collector Thank you.

Sandra *exits.*

Chris/Scrooge Bah humbug.

Annie/Fred Now, where is your clerk with that brandy?

Annie *opens the Maltesers box to reveal* **Robert** *holding up all the Maltesers behind him and holding a tray with three glasses.*

Robert/Clerk Three brandies, sir.

Chris *takes the brandies and closes the door on* **Robert.**

Robert (*quietly*) No please . . .

Chris *passes the glasses to* **Annie** *and* **Dennis**

Annie/Fred A toast to friends and family! Cheers!

Chris/Scrooge Cheers.

Dennis/Cratchit (*reading from the cup*)   IKEA!

They drink.

Chris/Scrooge Now, nephew, follow your new friend and be on your way!

Annie/Fred Only if you say you shall dine with us tomorrow.

Chris/Scrooge Every year you ask and every year my answer is the same. I bid you good afternoon.

Annie/Fred Merry Christmas, Uncle. God save you.

Christ/Scrooge Bah humbug.

Annie/Fred Bob, send my love to your family.

Dennis/Cratchit (*reads*)   Goodbye, Fred! Shakes hands.

Dennis *shakes his hands.*

Annie/Fred Goodbye.

Dennis/Cratchit (*reads*)   Mr Scrooge. I wanted to ask if I may take the day off tomorrow. If it's convenient, that is?

Chris/Scrooge   It is not convenient, Mr Cratchit.

Dennis/Cratchit   Oh Mr Scrooge, go to desk.

Dennis *goes to* **Scrooge**'s *desk and a drawer opens. He reads from inside.*

Dennis/Cratchit   Sir, I am not a rich man –

He reads along the desk and it leads him to the window.

Dennis/Cratchit   But if I can spend Christmas with my –

Jonathan *walks past the window carrying a Christmas present with FAMILY written on the side.*

Dennis/Cratchit   – family –

He continues along the wall.

– I would be content to . . .

Dennis *releases a roller blind over the window to reveal the word GNAW.*

Dennis/Cratchit   Gnaw!

Dennis *continues reading from a book* **Chris** *holds up.*

Dennis/Crachit   – upon a bone.

Chris/Scrooge   It's a poor excuse for picking a man's pocket every twenty-fifth of December. Give me one good reason for granting your request?

Reads from another stack of papers by **Scrooge**'s *desk.*

Dennis/Cratchit   Robert Grove acting CV page two.

Chris/Scrooge   Alright you've made your point.

Dennis/Cratchit   Lion King, nude. Role: Timon and Pubus.

Chris/Scrooge You may come to work one hour later but that is all.

Dennis *puts on glasses with BLESS and YOU written on the lenses.*

Dennis/Cratchit (*struggling to read*) Ouy Sselb!

Chris/Scrooge Bless you.

Dennis/Cratchit Thank you.

Dennis *exits and walks around the back of the shop passing by the window.*

Chris/Scrooge But make sure you are here all the earlier the next morning!

Dennis/Cratchit WANG!

Chris/Scrooge Bah humbug.

Chris *exits. Music plays and the lights shift. The backdrop is lowered down revealing* **Trevor** *pulling ropes in his gallery. He realises his mistake and pulls another rope, causing the office wall to fly out. He pulls another rope which flies out the chandelier. He then pulls the first rope to get the backdrop back in place.*

Scene 3 – LONDON STREET/SCROOGE'S FRONT DOOR

Chris *enters into the street. Three lampposts are set across the stage. One of them has been built with a bend/snap at the middle.*

Sandra/Narrator Scrooge walked back towards his lodgings, it was dark and cold –

SFX: Microwave beeps.

Through the backdrop we see the light of **Trevor***'s microwave and a meal revolving inside.*

Sandra/Narrator – his collar turned up against the icy wind.

Chris/Scrooge Trevor!

SFX: Bing!

The light goes out.

Sandra/Narrator The fog and darkness thickened, so that the ancient tower of the church became invisible and struck the hours and quarters in the clouds. As Scrooge made his way through the narrow streets and alleys, flecks of soft white snow began to fall.

Large gold coins begin falling from the rig. **Chris** *tries to avoid them, but keeps getting hit.*

Chris Argh! Argh!

A big clump of coins fall.

ARGH!

Max/Debtor Mr Scrooge, I beg a word, sir! Argh!

Chris/Scrooge What the devil is it, man?

Max/Debtor I've just received this notice of foreclosure but I am only a week behind, sir.

Chris/Scrooge And have you the money to pay?

Max *holds out his empty hands and piles of coins land in them.*

Max/Debtor Argh! Argh! No, I have nothing.

Chris *bats* **Max***'s hands down.*

Chris/Scrooge I do not write the law, sir, but I will live by it. Pay by the morning or your property will be sold.

Max/Debtor But it is Christmas Eve, sir, where will I find it? Money doesn't fall from the sky.

A large number of coins clatter down on top of them. **Max** *smiles briefly.*

Chris ARGH!

Max/Debtor Please, sir, think of my family!

Max *grabs* **Chris** *by the arm.*

Chris/Scrooge   You have kept me standing out in this snow long enough with your excuses! Leave me be.

Max *puts on a police hat and ducks behind* **Chris**.

Max/Policeman   Is this gent troubling you, sir?

Chris/Scrooge   Our business is concluded.

Max/Policeman   On your way then.

Chris/Scrooge   Thank you, Constable.

Max *switches back.*

Max/Debtor   Have a heart, Mr Scrooge!

Chris/Scrooge   Be gone!

Max/Policeman   Come on you!

He switches back and forth, arresting himself as he leaves.

Max/Debtor   No! Please!

Sandra *enters.*

Sandra/Narrator   Scrooge took his melancholy dinner in his usual melancholy tavern and went home to bed. He lived in chambers which had once belonged to his deceased partner. They were a gloomy suite of rooms, in a lowering pile of building up a yard. It was old enough now, and dreary enough, for nobody lived in it but Scrooge.

Chris *walks to his front door. On the door is a brass knocker in the shape of a face. Spooky music.*

Chris *searches for his keys and momentarily blocks the view of the knocker. When it is revealed again it has been swapped for* **Jonathan**'s *face, made up to look like the ghostly Jacob Marley.* **Chris** *jumps back startled.*

Chris/Scrooge   Jacob Marley?

Jonathan/Marley *Scrooooooo –*

– oooooge!

Jonathan/Marley *quickly replaces the normal knocker.* **Chris/Scrooge** *examines it.*

Chris/Scrooge   Humbug!

Sandra/Narrator   Scrooge, shaken by the vision, hurried inside.

Through the narration **Chris** *steps through the door and the wall piece rotates.* **Jonathan** *is caught in a contemporary dressing gown with his face painted bronze trying to climb out of the wardrobe. He ducks back inside.*

Sandra/Narrator   It was not his custom but feeling a shot of fear in his frosted heart Scrooge locked the door to his abode that night, and climbed the long winding staircase to his bedchamber.

The piece rotates the other way and this time **Jonathan** *is caught on the other side trying to climb out of the window. He hides again.*

Sandra/Narrator   Up Scrooge went, not caring a button for the darkness. Darkness is cheap, and Scrooge liked it. But before he shut his heavy door, he walked through his rooms to see that all was right. He had just enough recollection of the face to desire to do that. He looked about for signs of an intruder, but found none.

The piece rotates again and this time **Jonathan** *is caught on the other side trying to climb out of the window. He runs off stage spookily.*

Scene 4 – SCROOGE'S BED CHAMBER

A four-poster bed and window with curtains drawn.

Ominous music plays and we hear the clanking of chains from outside the window.

Sandra/Narrator   Scrooge retired for the night. Climbing into his four-poster, glad to finally get some sleep.

Chris *lies down on the bed:* **Robert** *emerges from the bedding,* **throwing** *Chris off the back of the bed.*

Robert/Scrooge   Humbug!

Chris/Scrooge   Robert!

Chris *runs around the bed and closes the curtains, shutting* **Robert** *inside the bed.*

Jonathan/Marley *(voice echoing)*   Scroooooooge!

Chris *climbs out of the bed.*

Chris/Scrooge   Who's there?

Jonathan/Marley   *Scrooooooge!*

Chris *pulls back the curtains revealing* **Jonathan** *(as the* **Ghost of Jacob Marley***) clinging to the window sill, terrified.*

Jonathan   Argh!!

Jonathan *climbs in.*

Chris/Scrooge   Who are you?

Jonathan/Marley   In life I was your partner Jacob Marley.

Chris/Scrooge   Humbug!

Jonathan/Marley   You don't believe in me?

Chris/Scrooge   I do not.

Jonathan/Marley   Why do you doubt your senses?

Chris/Scrooge   Because a little thing affects them. You may be an undigested bit of beef, a blot of mustard. There's more of gravy than the grave about you.

Jonathan *unwraps the bandages around his head and his jaw extends as he bellows at* **Chris**, *then replaces it.*

Jonathan/Marley   Arghh!

Chris/Scrooge   Mercy, dreadful apparition! Why do you trouble me.

Jonathan/Marley If a spirit goes not forth in life it is condemned to do so after death. Now I am doomed to wander through the world and witness what I cannot share.

Jonathan's *chain is caught on the chair.*

Chris/Scrooge Why are you bound, spirit?

Jonathan/Marley I wear the chain I forged in life! I made it link by link and yard by yard! I wear these lockboxes because they weigh me down with the money I coveted. I wear this chair because . . . I stole a chair, once. Don't steal chairs, Scrooge.

Trevor *enters and tries to unhook the chair.*

Jonathan/Marley I have no rest, no peace, only the endless pain of remorse.

Trevor *is now caught up in the chains.*

Trevor Oh no.

Jonathan/Marley I wear this angry man because . . . I stole the chair from him. Don't steal chairs, Scrooge!

Chris/Scrooge Humbug.

Jonathan/Marley Would you know the weight and length of the chain you bear yourself, Scrooge?

Chris/Scrooge I bear no chain.

Jonathan/Marley It was as heavy as this seven Christmases ago. Now it is a ponderous chain.

Jonathan *realises he is now chained to one of the posts of the bed.*

Jonathan/Marley I wear this four-poster bed because . . . it's very tiring dragging around a man and a chair.

Chris/Scrooge Be gone, spirit!

Jonathan/Marley Tonight you will be haunted by three spirits. Expect the first ghost when the bell tolls one.

SFX: Bell chiming once.

Not yet . . . When the bell tolls one . . . later on.

Jonathan *struggles to walk back towards the window, dragging the bed,* **Trevor** *and the chair.*

Chris/Scrooge   Can't I take them all at once and have it over with?

Jonathan/Marley   When the bell tolls one! When the bell tolls one! WHEN THE BELL TOLLS ONE!

Sandra *enters.*

Sandra/Narrator   The spirit faded silently into the mist.

Jonathan *exits into the wings, dragging the bed, chair and* **Trevor** *off with him, repeating 'When the bell tolls one' over and over until he's off stage.*

Sandra/Narrator   Scrooge climbed back into his bed.

Chris *irritably lies back down on the floor, he tucks himself in under a rug.*

Sandra/Narrator   And after a time, fell into a fitful sleep.

SFX: Bell chiming once.

Angelic choir music builds, full of foreboding. A light glows on the backcloth.

Annie/Past (*off*)   Scrooge . . .

Music, bright lights blinding the audience. Lights go down to reveal **Annie** *downstage as the* **Ghost of Christmas Past**. *Her costume consists of a pair of fake arms holding a candle in front of her, and a pair of fake crossed legs. Her real arms are operating a pair of flapping wings, and her real legs are disguised in dark black tights, creating the illusion of a hovering angelic creature.*

Annie/Past   Hello, Scrooge.

Chris/Scrooge   Are you the spirit whose coming was foretold to me?

Annie/Past   I am.

Chris/Scrooge   Who and what are you?

Annie/Past   I am the Ghost of Christmas Past. I shine with the light of a thousand Christmases gone. Take my hand and we shall journey through the mists of time.

Chris/Scrooge   Whither are we bound, spirit?

Annie/Past   The past Scrooge.

Chris/Scrooge   Long past?

Annie/Past   No, your past.

Chris *takes her hand and the scene changes around them.*

SFX: Whistling wind.

Annie *opens the wardrobe door, inside is light and smoke.*

Annie/Past   Step through the door, Scrooge, and into your past.

Chris *and* **Annie** *step into the wardrobe. The truck spins and* **Chris** *and* **Annie** *emerge into the school classroom, slightly dizzy.*

Scene 5 – SCHOOL HOUSE

Dennis (*as the* **School Master**) *wheels in a swivel chalkboard with the heading ALGEBRA and an equation below* $A^2 \times \pi \times \sqrt{5} =$

Annie/Past   What do you see on this Christmas Eve, Scrooge?

Chris/Scrooge (*rubbing his eyes*)   Why, it is my school master. Wise old Professor Tuddingly. A learned man he was indeed.

Max (*as* **Child Scrooge**) *enters.*

Annie/Past   Do you recognise this child?

Chris/Scrooge   It is me!

Max *smiles.*

Chris/Scrooge   What a solemn boy I was.

Max *pretends to scowl.*

Dennis/School Master   Now, boy, time to solve your equation. (*Reads.*) A. Small two. Kiss. Little house. Kiss. Snake under a table. Train tracks. And the answer is . . . Algeria.

Chris/Scrooge   I learned everything from that man.

Dennis *flips the board and we see the heading GEOMETRY with a diagram of a sphere with a dotted line around the circumference, a cone with a dotted line along the length and a cylinder.*

Dennis/School Master   And now . . . gimme-a-try. Ball with a belt. Party hat with a zip. Pringles. Good luck in your exams.

Chris/Scrooge   I so wish I could thank the Professor for all he did for me.

Annie/Past   Where were all the other boys?

Annie's *fake legs unfurl and flail around.*

Chris/Scrooge   At home with their families.

Annie/Past   And where were your family?

Chris/Scrooge   At home without me.

Annie/Past   Come, Scrooge, step through the door once again, there is more to see.

Music. **Chris** *goes back into the truck, smoke and light inside. The truck spins and* **Annie** *exits, leading* **Robert** *(as* **Scrooge***) by the hand.*

Robert/Scrooge   I know this place, spirit. It is the town I lived in as a young man.

Sandra *is wheeled on sitting on a park bench.*

Annie/Past   I see your heart grows light, but you still have not changed. Who is this?

Chris *opens the window, his hands tied with duck tape.*

Chris/Scrooge 'Tis Belle! Just as fair –

Robert *closes the window.*

Robert/Scrooge 'Tis Belle! Just as fair as I remember.

Chris *staggers out of the truck, tearing off the tape and shoves* **Robert** *back inside.*

Chris/Scrooge   Robert!

It is Belle! Just as fair as I remember.

Max *enters.*

Sandra/Belle   Please, Ebenezer, sit with me a while.

Max/Young Scrooge (*smiling*)   I must go back to work. If I am to save enough to buy the shop from Fezziwig then I cannot waste any time! The exchange is only open for another hour.

Sandra/Belle   Another idol has displaced me. One of gold and not of love that drives us both apart. Remember me, my darling . . . Russell.

Sandra *looks out knowingly to the reviewer.*

Max/Young Scrooge (*smiling*)   You don't mean that, do you Belle.

Sandra/Belle   I'm sorry, Ebenezer, we cannot be together any longer.

Max/Young Scrooge (*sadly*)   But Belle, my heart is broken. (*Grins.*) Nailed it!

Max *and* **Sandra** *exit and the bench is wheeled off.*

Chris/Scrooge   Spirit, please show me a happier time, I beg you!

Annie/Past   There is one Christmas I could show you that you may remember with more joy. A time when you yourself felt the warmth of human kindness.

Chris/Scrooge I will go willingly, spirit!

Chris *opens the door again revealing* **Robert** *with the axe.* **Chris** *slams the door closed.*

Chris/Scrooge Let's walk.

Scene 6 – SCROOGE'S SHOP

The walls of the shop are trucked back on and we find ourselves in Scrooge's shop but fifty years in the past, back when Mr Fezziwig was the proprietor. The shop looks brighter and cleaner and is decorated for Christmas. The gigantic box of Maltesers still stands stage right. **Jonathan** *(as Mr Fezziwig) sets decorations.* **Dennis** *sets a Christmas tree, as he plugs it in the starcloth at the back begins to malfunction. Half of it falls down to reveal* **Trevor** *eating in his gallery.*

Chris *and* **Annie** *look on through the window centre stage.* **Sandra** *re-enters from the wing.*

Sandra/Narrator Scrooge was transported to his shop but not as he knew it.

Dennis *plugs in the Christmas Tree which causes the lights to flicker and buzz.*

Sandra/Narrator Gone were the stacks of yellowing papers and the ledgers filled with debtors' names. And the dusty chandelier shone with its former brilliance once more.

Trevor *pulls a rope and the chandelier lowers into view.*

Chris/Scrooge Why, it's old Fezziwig, alive again, God bless him and preparing for his Christmas ball.

Annie/Past A small matter to make these silly folks so full of gratitude.

Chris/Scrooge A small matter indeed.

Chris *is suddenly yanked out of sight and* **Robert** *takes his place.*

Robert/Scrooge A small matter indeed!

Chris *reappears and shoves* **Robert** *off again.* **Dennis** *enters (as* **Young Marley**) *with a ledger.*

Annie/Past And who comes now, Scrooge!

Chris/Scrooge Why, it is Jacob Marley. But scarce a day over twenty-five. We both apprenticed with old Fezziwig.

Chris *pushes* **Robert** *out of sight.*

Jonathan/Fezziwig Young Marley, no more work for tonight. Come, pull a cracker with me.

Jonathan *and* **Dennis** *pull a cracker.* **Dennis** *reads the note inside.*

Dennis/Cratchit No, thank you. I still have work to do.

Jonathan/Fezziwig No more work, Jacob, our guests are starting to arrive.

Jonathan *opens the door to reveal* **Sandra** *and* **Trevor** *(as* **Mr** *and* **Mrs Potterby**).

Sandra/Mrs Potterby Merry Christmas, my dear Fezziwig!

Jonathan/Fezziwig Season's greetings, Mrs Potterby!

Sandra/Mrs Potterby I wish to thank you most sincerely for the extra ten shillings.

Jonathan/Fezziwig Oh, pish-posh!

Sandra/Mrs Potterby When I saw you had left it on my table I was overwhelmed. (*Overwhelmed face.*) Then I was worried there had been a mistake. (*Worried face.*) But then my heart filled with joy. (*Joyful face.*) And bafflement. (*Baffled face.*) How did you feel, Mr Potterby?

Trevor/Mr Potterby Yeah, fine.

Jonathan/Fezziwig Enjoy the festivities!

Sandra *and* **Trevor** *enter the party.* **Max** *enters.*

Jonathan/Fezziwig Ah! The Bodkin family is here. Bertie!

Jonathan *shakes* **Max**'s *hand four times.*

Max/Bertie   Hello!

Jonathan/Fezziwig   Arthur.

Max/Arthur   Hello!

Jonathan/Fezziwig   And Freddy!

Max/Freddy   Hello!

Jonathan/Fezziwig   And the finest fiddle player in London, Claude Monnier.

Max/Claude (*deep voice*)   Bonsoir.

Max *crosses to the corner where the musicians will play.* **Chris** *and* **Annie** *appear downstage left.*

Annie *has now tied her fake legs in a knot.*

Chris/Scrooge   They do all so admire the old man.

Annie/Past   What is the matter, Scrooge?

Chris/Scrooge   I should like to be able to say a word or two to my clerk just now.

Annie/Past   Then we had best leave this place, Scrooge.

Chris/Scrooge   Nay, spirit.

Robert *opens the door hitting* **Chris** *and*

Robert/Scrooge   Nay, spirit! Let me remain –

Chris *pushes the door closed again and locks it, shutting* **Robert** *out of the room.*

Chris/Scrooge   LET ME REMAIN! The night's revelry is about to begin.

Jonathan *steps forward to address the room.*

Jonathan/Fezziwig   Welcome, dear friends, to the grand Fezziwig Christmas Ball!

SFX: 10,000 people cheering. It stops abruptly.

Jonathan/Fezziwig It brings me such joy to look around the room and see so many happy faces.

Sandra *does a happy face.*

Jonathan/Fezziwig Mr Monnier, let us have some music!

Max *mimes playing his violin. SFX: Deck the Halls trumpet solo. After the first phrase more brass comes in.*

Jonathan/Fezziwig Wonderful! Wonderful! Now let us all dance!

All *perform random knee bends. Song ends.*

Jonathan/Fezziwig Tremendous! And if it isn't young Master Scrooge.

Max *runs to the door and re-enters (with hat) as* **Young Scrooge**.

Jonathan/Fezziwig Merry Christmas, Ebenezer.

Max/Young Scrooge Fezziwig.

Jonathan/Fezziwig Let me take your hat.

Jonathan *takes* **Max**'s *hat and calls over his shoulder.*

Jonathan/Fezziwig Bertie, hang this will you.

Max *runs around* **Jonathan** *and takes the hat.*

Max/Bertie Yes, sir.

Max *runs back around* **Jonathan**.

Jonathan/Fezziwig Thank you.

Max *puts the hat back on.*

Jonathan/Fezziwig Now, Ebenezer, how about a spot of my favourite brandy?

Jonathan *quickly climbs up a few steps on the ladder, reaching for the brandy.*

Jonathan/Fezziwig Argh! Argh! ARGHH!!

Jonathan *immediately climbs back down without the brandy.*

Jonathan/Fezziwig Yummy.

Jonathan *crosses to the other guests.* **Max** *goes to* **Dennis**.

Max/Young Scrooge The old fool thinks me his loyal apprentice. I have come from the Exchange, Jacob. His shop will be ours before the New Year.

Chris/Scrooge Let us go, spirit, I can watch no more of this!

Annie/Past But, Scrooge . . . the night's revelry is about to begin.

Max/Young Scrooge Fezziwig!

Max *strides over to* **Jonathan**. *The other guests look over.*

Max/Young Scrooge I have come from a meeting with your former partner. He and I have an agreement. Read the contract, Jacob.

Dennis/Young Marley Noah's Ark show report. Badgers contained: three. Badgers loose: six.

Jonathan/Fezziwig Well, I wasn't expecting to hear that.

Max/Young Scrooge There you have it. Sneersby is to buy out your stake in the firm and Marley and I will run it for him. Your services will no longer be required.

SFX: Music, dramatic/turbulent.

Jonathan/Fezziwig No, please, Ebenezer!

Sandra/Mrs Potterby My heart breaks for Fezziwig!

Sandra *pulls her most emotional face yet.*

Chris/Scrooge Spirit, let me leave this place!

Chris *as* **Scrooge** *moves centre looking for a way out but the characters at the party circle him and address him directly.*

Sandra/Mrs Potterby   Your behaviour is completely unacceptable, Mr Scrooge.

Trevor/Mr Potterby   If you keep on like this you'll end up with no friends, no one who cares for you and no place in society.

Dennis/Marley (*reading*)   Badgers contained: one. Badgers loose: eight. Patrons dead: three.

Jonathan/Fezziwig   We're all trying to get into the Christmas spirit, Ebenezer, and you've ruined it.

Sandra/Mrs Potterby   No wonder his last firm slung him out.

Chris   No! NO! NO! I'M NOT SCROOGE!

Silence.

Annie   What?

Robert *appears in the flying gallery.*

Robert   No! I'm Scrooge!

Robert *releases a rope and drops the chandelier onto* **Chris**. **Chris** *dives out the way, causing a domino effect.*

1 – **Chris** *knocks into* **Annie**.

2 – **Annie** *falls over pushing* **Max** *on the ladder.*

3 – The ladder slides stage right sending **Max** *into the Maltesers box which tips back, the bottom opens and giant Maltesers spill out all over the stage.*

4 – **Trevor** *and* **Jonathan** *stumble on the Maltesers and fall, both grabbing the chandelier rope to try and save themselves.*

5 – The pull on the rope propels **Robert** *(who is still holding the other end) into the rig (this is a dummy/form switched in).*

6 – **Robert** *(second dummy) lands on an LX bar stage right, the bar tips and* **Robert** *slides stage right to stage left down the tilted LX bar, lamps falling off the bar as he goes.*

*7 – **Robert** crashes into the DSL house with a loud splintering sound, the front falls down to reveal **Robert** (the actor) wedged through the wood.*

*8 – A giant version of **Robert**'s acting CV falls down from the rig, **Robert**'s headshot is next to **Robert**. **Robert** assumes the same pose as the headshot.*

Blackout.

INTERVAL

Trevor *walks around the auditorium with a big net, collecting in the giant Maltesers.*

The CV remains in view during the interval so the audience can read the various credits listed.

Part III

PERFORMANCE

Chris (Over Speaker) Welcome back to the second half of A Christmas Carol. After a positive creative conversation, it has been agreed that the role of Ebeneezer Scrooge will continue to be played by Chris Bean.

Robert (Over Speaker) That is not what we agreed, Chris!

Chris (Over Speaker) Get in the box, Robert! And now, a performance from the Cornley Handbell Choir who are delighted be performing today with only one bell missing.

Scene 1 – SCROOGE'S BED CHAMBER

Annie, **Dennis**, **Trevor**, **Jonathan** and **Max** *perform Good King Wenceslas on handbells. The clapper falls out of one of* **Trevor**'s *handbells and he begins saying 'ding' to replace that note.*

Sandra/Narrator The second hour was nearly upon him and Scrooge lay awake in his bed, unable to sleep a wink, awaiting the second spirit.

Lights up on **Chris** *(as* **Scrooge***) lying in the four-poster bed. On the other side of the room is a giant gift box. Clock chimes two.* **Sandra** *exits. Christmas bells ring and music builds.*

Robert/Present (*inside the box*) Ho! Ho! Ho!

We hear a loud thump inside the box as **Robert** *tries to stand up.*

Robert/Present Urgh. Shit!

Robert *bangs on the top of the gift box.*

Robert/Present Come on! Eeear!

Silence.

Greetings!

Chris/Scrooge Who are you, spirit?

Robert/Present I am the Ghost of Christmas Present! Look upon me.

Chris *gets out of bed.*

Robert/Present I am laughter, I am joy, I am Christmas! Come and know me better man.

Chris/Scrooge Conduct me where you will and I shall profit from the lesson you have.

Robert/Present I have much to show you and we will learn much together. Follow me to the window! Err. Follow me to the window! Follow me to the window! Follow me to the window!

Robert *tips his box over, moving slowly towards the window.*

Robert/Present Urgh! Holly wreath! Urgh! Urgh! Are we there?

Chris/Scrooge No.

Robert/Present Ah. We have much to learn.

Robert *punches his legs out through the base of the box.*

Robert/Present Help me up!

Robert *is helped up.*

Robert/Present This way!

Robert *strides confidently into* **Chris**, *knocking him down.*

Chris/Scrooge Argh!

Robert *helps* **Chris** *up.*

Robert/Present There is much to see. Take my hand.

Beat.

Chris/Scrooge How?

Robert/Present Touch my thigh.

Chris/Scrooge No.

Robert/Present Just touch my thigh.

Chris/Scrooge I'm not touching your thigh.

Robert/Present Just do it.

Sandra *enters.*

Sandra/Narrator And so Scrooge did as he was told and touched the spirit's thigh.

Chris *touches* **Robert**'s *thigh.*

Chris/Scrooge It's wet.

Robert/Present Of course it is, I'm boiling. I've been in here the whole interval.

Chris/Scrooge Let's just go.

Robert/Present Onward!

Scene 2 – LONDON STREET

Robert *and* **Chris** *walk down the street.* **Max, Sandra** *and* **Jonathan** *are passing through (as* passers-by*).* **Robert** *knocks into them.*

All Argh! Argh!

Chris/Scrooge Where are you taking me, spirit?

Robert/Present Ho! Ho! Ho! To see those who love you most Scrooge. For too long you have kept Christmas alone, trapped inside. You should be like me and share the joy of Christmas with those around you and sup upon the milk of human kindness.

The continue on their journey through the street.

Part III, Scene 3   63

Robert/Present   Whose house is this?

Chris/Scrooge   Why it is Fred, my nephew. He holds a Christmas Party every year.

Robert/Present   Let us see how they keep Christmas.

Scene 3 – FRED'S HOUSE

Kelly's Dreamhouse, pink walls with pink counters and furniture.

Annie/Fred   Season's greetings one and all.

Jonathan/Topper   Fred, you've outdone yourself with the decorations. Edwards, fetch me a sherry will you.

Max/Edwards (*smiling*)   Yes, sir.

Max *opens a cupboard triggering a V/O from the house.*

Kelly V/O   Let's bake cookies.

Max *offers him a plate of plastic cookies.*

Max/Edwards   Your sherry, sir.

Jonathan/Topper   Superb.

He gnaws on a plastic cookie.

Annie/Fred   The food smells absolutely divine.

Max/Edwards   That's the ham, sir.

Max *opens the microwave door.*

Kelly V/O   Mmm! Fresh cinnamon buns!

Max *takes out a plate of plastic cinnamon buns.*

Max/Edwards   The braised ham, sir. Allow me to carve.

Jonathan/Topper   Thank you, Edwards, now come along, one more game before we eat. Let's play guess!

Annie/Fred   Alright. I've got one!

Max/Edwards Is it vegetable?

Annie/Fred Not vegetable, no.

Jonathan/Topper Mineral then?

Robert/Present Chris, there's no air in here.

Chris/Scrooge Quiet.

Annie/Fred Not mineral. No.

Max/Edwards Animal!

Robert/Present I can't breathe, Chris.

Chris/Scrooge Shh!

Robert/Present For God's sake. (*Getting louder.*) I'll turn the microphone down. (*Loud.*) My balls are absolutely sodden.

Annie/Fred Animal it is!

Jonathan/Topper Is it alive?

Annie/Fred More or less.

Robert/Present I need to get out of this robe.

Chris/Scrooge Robert!

Robert/Present I'm panicking! Cut me a breathing hole!

Chris/Scrooge Fine.

Chris *picks up a knife from the counter and tries to cut a hole. The plastic can't pierce the box.*

Robert/Present Come on! Harder!

Trevor *enters with a flick-knife and stabs it into the box.*

Robert/Present Argh! Right in the tit!

Jonathan/Topper This animal. Is it disagreeable or friendly?

Annie/Fred Disagreeable for sure.

Max/Edwards Does it growl?

Annie/Fred Sometimes.

Robert/Present Urgh. Urgh. Urgh.

Chris/Scrooge Quiet!

Jonathan/Topper I know –

Robert/Present I'm burning up! Get me in the fridge!

Robert kicks open the door to the fridge and puts his leg inside.

Robert/Present Oh God, it's not even real!

Chris/Scrooge Shut up, Robert.

Robert/Present You shut up! It should be you in this box! I should be Scrooge! My son's watching this! Fleance are you out there?!

He looks into the audience. No one responds.

Robert/Present He's gone! Nooooo!

He falls to his knees.

Jonathan/Topper I know what it is! A disagreeable creature but none of these, it is your uncle. Ebenezer Scrooge.

Annie/Fred It is! It is!

Robert/Present Help me up!

They struggle to get him to his feet.

Do what you can! Do what you can!

Annie/Fred I do so wish that he would join us for Christmas.

SFX: Doorbell.

Max/Edwards Perhaps that is your uncle now?

Annie *opens a cabinet to reveal a decal of 'Chip' in beach wear.*

Chip V/O Hey ladies, want to play kissy kissy?

Annie/Fred Just carollers.

Max/Edwards Er . . . Would you like to play kissy kissy, sir?

Jonathan/Topper No Edwards, not before lunch. Or after.

Annie/Fred Oh poor Uncle Scrooge, I hate to think of him all alone.

Jonathan/Topper You extend a warm invitation to him every Christmas.

Annie/Fred Yes, but for some reason he never wants to come.

Annie *leans sadly on the wall and accidentally presses a button.*

Beach DJ V/O Party time!

LX: Disco lights flash.

Beach DJ *(another decal) emerges out of a counter top with a mixing deck.*

SFX: Dance music plays.

The **Beach DJ**'s *mouth moves robotically as the voiceover plays.*

Beach DJ V/O (*sings*) Ooh Kelly let's have fun! Let's go dancing in the sun!

Annie *frantically presses buttons on the wall to try and stop the music.*

Beach DJ V/O Let's make this a pool party!

Bubbles spray out of the set as more lights flash.

Beach DJ V/O (*sings*) Ooh Kelly splash and play! Having fun the Kelly way!

Annie *presses more buttons.*

Beach DJ V/O Language settings – French – Italian – German – (*Sings.*) Ooh Kelly, komm wir gehn! Tanzen fröhlich in der sonn!

Jonathan *pushes the* **Beach DJ** *back down into the counter and the music, lights and bubbles stop.*

The drawer closes.

Jonathan/Topper   I can't imagine why he wouldn't want to visit.

Annie/Fred   Uncle Scrooge may be gruff and grim but I for one feel sorry for the old man. I will not be angry with him.

Jonathan/Topper   Then you are a better man than he.

The **Beach DJ** *bursts out of the counter again.*

Beach DJ V/O   DAS IST FUNKTASTIC!

Jonathan, Max *and* **Annie** *force him back down again and exit.*

Scene 4 – LONDON STREET

Chris/Scrooge   A disagreeable creature? Gruff and grim? Is that really what they think of me?

Robert/Present   Look not back, Scrooge! Nor worry what the future may hold. Be like me and stay in the present.

Chris/Scrooge   Where next torturous spirit?

Robert/Present   Touch my thigh once more.

Chris *touches* **Robert**'s *thigh again.*

Robert/Present   On to another house this Christmas Day. Do you recognise this abode, Scrooge?

Scene 5 – THE CRATCHIT'S HOUSE

The house is simple and scarcely furnished. (A wooden table, chairs, fireplace and window.) **Sandra** *(as* **Mrs Cratchit**) *is finishing setting the table for Christmas dinner.*

Chris/Scrooge 'Tis Bob Cratchit's house to be sure.

Robert/Present Let us see how the Cratchit's keep Christmas.

Dennis (as **Bob Cratchit**) *enters carrying a tray with glasses and a bottle. He reads off of a glass.*

Dennis/Cratchit (*reads*) Merry Christmas, my darling. When you have finished laying the table take a seat and warm yourself by the –

Sandra *takes her glass and* **Dennis** *stops speaking. She hands the glass back.*

Dennis/Cratchit (*reads*) – fire. Now set down the tray and stand on the red cross.

Dennis *searches around for a red mark. Eventually he finds it where he was standing. He takes a large wine bottle and reads.*

Dennis/Cratchit Wine, my love?

Moves to the table.

Sandra/Mrs Cratchit Just a drop.

Dennis *up ends the bottle to read from the base, pouring wine everywhere.* **Sandra** *tries to catch the liquid in various glasses on the table.*

Dennis/Cratchit Tiny Tim was as good as gold this morning. He told me that he hoped that others in the church would see him so that they may be reminded who made lame beggars walk and blind men see. Enough wine for you, my dear?

Sandra/Mrs Cratchit Plenty.

Dennis/Cratchit Cheers!

Sandra/Mrs Cratchit Cheers. What are we having for dinner, Bob?

Dennis *looks at the duck, slowly rotating on the fire.*

Sandra/Mrs Cratchit   Bob?

The duck turns around to reveal the word DUCK written on the back. **Dennis** *ducks.* **Sandra** *drags him back to his feet.*

Sandra/Mrs Cratchit   What are we having for dinner, Bob?

Dennis *takes off his hat and reads a line from inside.*

Dennis/Cratchit   Tiny Tim.

Sandra/Mrs Cratchit   Sounds delicious! When will it be ready?

Reads paper from pocket.

Dennis/Cratchit   January twelfth. Court Summons. Trevor Watson. Dangerous driving of yellow transit van.

Sandra/Mrs Cratchit   Very good. I pray for our Tim, it seems he grows more frail by the day. Oh, here he comes now!

SFX. Thunderously loud footsteps. **Sandra** *and* **Dennis** *look out, full of fear.*

Sandra/Mrs Cratchit   Tiny Tim?

A huge puppet head of **Mr Garibaldi** *bangs against the window outside the house.*

Sandra/Mrs Cratchit   Arghhh!

Tiny Tim (*deep voice*)   MOTHER. FATHER.

Sandra/Mrs Cratchit   There's my boy . . .

Chris/Scrooge   Merciful Lord, I've never seen such a delicate child.

Tiny Tim   HAPPY CHRISTMAS.

Sandra/Mrs Cratchit   Come and give me a hug.

Tiny Tim   I SHALL.

Tiny Tim's *giant hand reaches in through the door and clumsily hits* **Sandra**.

Sandra/Mrs Cratchit Ahh! Will you take a little food, Tiny Tim? You must keep your strength up!

Tiny Tim YES, MAMA.

Tiny Tim's *hand smashes the table, knocking all the cutlery and crockery to the floor.*

Dennis *pushes the hand out of the door, slams it closed and then shuts the blind.*

Dennis/Cratchit Tiny Tim, come and sit upon your mother's lap.

Sandra/Mrs Cratchit No, Tim! The cold night air is good for your constitution.

Dennis/Cratchit How about a little duck?

Tiny Tim's *head appears above the kitchen.*

Tiny Tim YES PLEASE. FEED. ME.

Robert *screams, tries to run offstage but instead slams into a set piece, falling to the ground.*

Dennis *opens the window and tosses the whole duck into* **Tiny Tim**'s *mouth.*

Tiny Tim MAY I HAVE SOME MORE?

Sandra/Mrs Cratchit I'm afraid that's all we have, though I wish I could give you more. I know you have been unwell of late.

Tiny Tim I FEEL MOST FRAIL.

Sandra/Mrs Cratchit There, there, Tim!

The kettle whistles. **Tiny Tim**'s *mouth opens giving the impression he is screaming.*

Tiny Tim NOW LET US TOAST MR SCROOGE.

His eyes roll into the back of his head.

Sandra/Mrs Cratchit It's because of that uncaring man that you are suffering. I will not raise my glass.

Dennis/Cratchit Do as he says!

His eyes roll back in and stare at **Sandra**.

Tiny Tim MR SCROOGE IS A GOOD MAN. WE OWE HIM ALL WE HAVE.

His eyes move slowly from side to side.

Sandra/Mrs Cratchit What a generous and kind little soul you are.

Tiny Tim GOD BLESS US. EVERYONE.

Scene 6 – LONDON STREET

Chris *and* **Robert** *continue on their way.*

Chris/Scrooge Tell me, spirit. Will Tiny Tim live?

Robert/Present I hope not. I see a vacant seat and a crutch without an owner. If these shadows remain unchanged the massive child will die.

Chris/Scrooge Spirit, how can I make that change? Show me. Please?

Robert/Present What then? If he be like to die he had better do it, and decrease the surplus population.

Beat.

Our time grows short and I must depart.

Chris/Scrooge Will you leave me so alone?

Robert/Present Before you go, you must sup upon the milk of human kindness. Drink from my chalice.

Chris/ Scrooge ... How?

Robert *squats down and a small chalice pops out from the bottom of the present.*

Robert/Present There you go. I'd give that a rinse if I were you. Goodbye, Scrooge.

Robert *tries to walk directly off the front of the stage,* **Chris** *catches him.* **Jonathan**, **Annie**, **Dennis** *and* **Max** *run onstage to herd* **Robert** *off into the wing.*

Robert/Present I think that went very well.

Chris *is left alone.*

Chris/Scrooge Spirit! Please come back, show me where to go!

SFX. Eerie music.

Lights shift. **Trevor** *(as* **Ghost of Christmas Yet to Come***) appears stage right wearing a tall and unwieldy hooded costume. He slowly makes his way towards* **Chris**. *As he moves he makes a scary 'moaning sound' which echoes around the stage.*

SFX: Car alarm.

The headlights of **Trevor**'s *van flash, shining through the backdrop.* **Trevor** *hurriedly searches his pockets, finds his keys and turns off the alarm, then continues walking.*

Chris/Scrooge I am in the presence of the Ghost of Christmas Yet to Come?

Trevor *slowly nods his head which sags slightly downstage. A long skeletal hand reaches out towards* **Chris** *motioning for him to follow.*

Chris/Scrooge I fear you more than any spectre I have seen. But as I know your purpose is to do me good I shall hear this new lesson with a thankful heart. Will you not speak to me?

The skeletal hand points again. **Trevor** *sneezes, dropping the arm.*

Chris/Scrooge Bless you.

Trevor/Ghost Ah no.

His own hand sticks out of the costume and fumbles around to retrieve the prop arm/hand.

Chris/Scrooge Lead on! The night is waning fast, and it is precious time to me, I know. Lead on, spirit!

Trevor *points as* **Max** *(as the* **Debtor** *from earlier) enters.*

Max/Debtor My love! My love, I have wonderous news!

Max *turns to reveal he's wearing a half and half costume.*

Max/Mary What news, my sweet?

Max/Debtor The old man is no more!

Max/Mary No more? You mean he is dead?

Max/Debtor As dead as a doornail, my love! Alfred come in here, my son!

Max *holds up a sock puppet.*

Max/Alfred What is it, father?

Max/Debtor Our worries are over! Our debt is cleared.

Max/Mary Cleared and cleared for good!

Max/Alfred Oh father! Grandmama will be so pleased.

Max *reveals another sock puppet.*

Max/Grandmama Oh happy day! I have waited for this moment for two score years and ten!

Max/Debtor But how wrong it feels to revel in another's demise.

Max/Mary But that crook has caused us naught but pain.

Max/Alfred 'Tis true, father!

Max/Grandmama That scoundrel shall not be missed.

Max/Mary And we may keep our savings.

Max/Debtor And do good with them too!

Max/Alfred Great Grandpa's medicine!

Max *tears open his shirt front revealing a big Great Grandpa face.*

Max/Great Grandpa I am saved!

Max/Alfred We may keep Patches and Scruff!

Max *pulls out two small dog puppets and shakes them.*

Max/Dogs Woof! Woof! Woof!

Max/Debtor Oh what joy! That wicked man is dead and our family is saved!

Max *grins, takes a big bow and runs off.*

Chris/Scrooge Such a vibrant family. Who is the wretched soul of which this family speaks? How cruel must he be for them to celebrate his passing so. I see, I see. The case of this unhappy man might be my own.

Trevor *points and beckons for* **Chris** *to follow.*

He slowly makes his way across the stage whacking his head against the Dead Duck sign which swings back and hits him again. He gets tangled in a warehouse pulley and yanks himself free.

Scene 7 – GRAVEYARD OF ST BARNABUS

Several free-standing headstones are placed about the stage and a pair of wrought iron gates with large letters reading **Graveyard of St Barnabus** *on the arch.* **Dennis** *stands on small stone plinth* *dressed as a statue of a cherub.* **Jonathan** *stands on a higher plinth, quivering with fear.*

Chris/Scrooge   Spirit, whither do you take me?

Trevor *tries to enter through the archway but he's too tall to fit through. He bangs his hooded head on the top of the arch and various letters fall off so the sign ends up reading G A Y BAR.* **Chris** *and* **Trevor** *finally make it through the arch.*

Chris/Scrooge   Why have you brought me here to . . . the gay bar . . .

Trevor (*as the* **Ghost**) *again signals with his long arm, he goes to point at one of the headstones but his arm falls off. He tries to pick it up with the other long arm (using it like a kind of shovel) but can only push it along the floor. He bends down to pick it up but accidentally knocks one of the headstones over triggering a domino effect where all the headstones fall over. He tries to pick them up but just knocks into other bits of the set making things worse. He stumbles and knocks* **Jonathan** *off his plinth before falling over himself. He flails around on the ground before* **Dennis** *helps him back up. They quickly reset the gravestones.*

Chris/Scrooge   Spirit! This is a fearful place. In leaving it, I shall not leave its lesson, trust me. Let us go!

Trevor *points again.*

Chris/Scrooge   Please, spirit. Before I draw nearer to that stone to which you point, answer me one question. Are these the shadows of the things that will be, or are they shadows of things that May be, only?

Trevor *points again.*

Chris/Scrooge   Tell me, what wretched name adorns that grave?

LX: Flash of lightning and a spotlight comes up on one of the now mixed up graves. Lightning flashes and the spotlight comes up to reveal it reads **Chris Bean** *with* **Ebenezer Scrooge** *written in the gaps.*

SFX/LX: Thunder and lightning.

Chris/Scrooge Chris Ebenezer Bean Scrooge. That's almost my name! Am I the wretched soul who lies cold and dead in ... the gay bar?

SFX: Moaning.

SFX/LX: Thunder and lightning.

Chris/Scrooge Oh dreadful apparition, please tell me that I may change these shadows by an altered life.

Trevor/Ghost of Christmas Yet to Come Aye, laddie ...

Chris/Scrooge I will learn my lesson, I swear it! Please spirit! Please!

Robert *and* **Annie** *run on holding crow puppets on long sticks.* **Robert** *takes the opportunity to hit* **Chris** *with his crow.*

Jonathan *and* **Dennis** *pull* **Chris** *to his knees, driving him into his own grave.*

SFX: Spooky building music and blowing winds.

Sandra *enters.*

Sandra/Narrator Scrooge descended deep into his own grave, his cries for mercy ignored by the spirt.

Chris/Scrooge No! No! No!

Chris *exits.*

Scene 8 – SCROOGE'S BED CHAMBER

Sandra/Narrator But no sooner did he feel the cold earth against his skin he realised he had been transported back to his chambers and found himself safely wrapped up in his bed.

Sandra *exits. After a moment the bed is quickly wheeled back on. It stops abruptly and* **Chris** *shoots out hitting the ground. He jumps back onto the mattress and closes the four poster curtains.* **Chris** *pulls back the curtains.*

Chris/Scrooge   What is this? I am saved. O, Jacob Marley be praised! I am alive!

Chris *closes the door.* **Chris** *runs to his window and throws it open.*

Chris/Scrooge   You there!

Dennis *enters as a* **Young Boy**.

Chris/Scrooge   Yes, you boy. Tell me, what day is it?

Dennis (*says the current weekday, e.g.*)   Friday.

Chris/Scrooge   No, it's Christmas Day!

Dennis/Boy   Oh, I've not done my shopping!

Dennis *starts to run off.*

Chris/Scrooge   No! No, come back! Boy, run to the butcher's and use these ten shillings to –

Chris *opens another coin purse and more snow is inside.*

Chris/Scrooge   It's snow again! Take this snow to the butcher's and use it to buy the biggest goose they have. You'll have to negotiate, but get the goose and bring it straight to my shop and here, take another ten shillings for your –

He opens another coin purse of snow becoming more furious.

Chris/Scrooge   It's more snow! Take this snow for your trouble! You are welcome to it.

Dennis *jogs over to* **Chris** *and takes the coin purse full of snow.*

Dennis/Boy   Thanks.

Dennis *exits.*

Chris/Scrooge   *Oh happy day!* The spirits be blessed for I am born again.

SFX: Uplifting and swelling music as we transition back to the shop.

Scene 9 – LONDON STREET/FRED'S HOUSE

Dennis *(as* **Bob Cratchit***) enters wearing a winter coat. He reads his lines from an incredibly long scarf wrapped around his neck.* **Robert** *(as* **Lamplighter***) is also there.*

Dennis/Cratchit Sorry I'm late, Mr Scrooge. I was making merry with my family. I promise to make up the time this evening if you'll accept my apology.

Chris/Scrooge No, Bob. This is completely unacceptable.

Dennis/Cratchit Please, sir, I -

Chris/Scrooge It is unacceptable, that a man should work at all on Christmas Day. It is I that must apologise to you.

Dennis *reads from* **Annie***'s minutes book.*

Dennis/Cratchit Mr Scrooge?

Chris/Scrooge Gather around, everyone!

Max *(with an element of costume from all of the parts he's played)* and **Sandra** *(as* **Collector***), ensemble as* **Passers-by***.*

Chris/Scrooge I have treated all of you unkindly and I wish to make amends. Bob, you have worked your fingers to the bone in this office for more years than I can count but I have always paid you poorly. Yesterday when you asked if you could have Christmas Day off I cold-heartedly refused. Bob, you shall have the day off, nay, the whole week.

All Huzzah!

Chris/Scrooge What say you to that, Bob?

Dennis *reads from* **Annie***'s minutes book.*

Dennis/Cratchit (*reads*) Page three. Minutes from previous production meeting continued. 7:04 Robert says: 'No one tell Chris that we're doing secret production meetings'. Sandra says: 'That man really is a complete arse'. All nod in agreement. 7:05 Max chuckles. Jonathan says: 'Maybe he's just method acting as Scrooge'. Trevor replies: 'Nah mate, he's just not a good guy at all'. Jonathan says: 'Can we get back on topic. These meetings are always so rudderless'. Max replies: 'Yeah, like a cow'. Jonathan replied: 'But cows do have udders'. Max replied: 'Mine doesn't'. Trevor replied: 'That's because it's a dog'. Sandra said: 'Please stop this conversation. We're getting off topic. The reason we're all here is to talk about what we're going to do about Chris'. 7:06 Robert said: 'He stole Scrooge from me'. Dennis said: 'He's been really horrible'. Robert said: 'All in favour of staging a coup'. Max replied: 'A Scottish cow?' Robert said: 'No! A coup. After Christmas Carol we're kicking Chris out of the Society. All in favour? The vote is unanimous. Max, stop laughing.'

Trevor *snatches* **Dennis***'s file away. Silence.* **Chris** *hands him another file.*

Dennis/Cratchit A whole week off! Mrs Cratchit will be so glad to have me home for Christmas.

Chris/Scrooge Will she? Well, TOUGH TITTIES!

Dennis/Cratchit What?

Chris/Scrooge You're not going home for Christmas at all! You're going to work Cratchit, you're going work until you bleed!

Robert/Clerk But Mr Scrooge –

Chris/Scrooge Yes. I've had a change of change of heart.

You're all just a bunch of greedy, conniving, back-stabbing knobs! You don't deserve my generosity.

Sandra/Collector But Mr Scrooge, don't you want to make a donation to the poor?

Chris/Scrooge Sod the poor. In fact, give me back my snow.

Chris *snatches a handful of snow from her collection tin.*

Sandra/Collector But what about the needy –

Chris/Scrooge What they need is to get a job and stop scrounging. Scrooge works hard for his money, why shouldn't he keep it? I pay my taxes don't I? Everyone just wants a bloody handout because it's Christmas. Well, look after number one, that's the lesson I've learned.

An ensemble member enters with the goose.

Chris/Scrooge Ah, the goose. Give that to me. Off we go to Fred's House.

Kelly's Dreamhouse trucks on with **Annie** *(as* **Fred***) and* **Jonathan** *(as* **Topper***).*

Annie/Fred Uncle! You've come home for Christmas.

Jonathan/Topper Merry Christmas, Mr Scrooge.

Chris/Scrooge Shut up, irrelevant character.

Annie/Fred And you have brought a goose.

Chris/Scrooge Oh yes! Smells good, doesn't it, Fred?

Annie/Fred Oh yes.

Chris/Scrooge It's mine. I'm going to sit here and eat this entire goose and you're all going to watch.

Annie/Fred Oh.

Chris *sits down and starts eating.*

Chris/Scrooge Mmmm. Mmmm.

Robert/Clerk   Chris, I think it's made of Styrofoam.

Chris/Scrooge   It's my Styrofoam! Bring in Tiny Tim, I want him to watch me eat my goose while he starves!

Chris *chokes on the fake goose, he stands and coughs, bumping into the dreamhouse, the* **Beach DJ** *pops up.*

Beach DJ V/O   Das Ist Partyzeit!

Disco music. **Chris** *hits the* **DJ** *and breaks the dreamhouse, the music and his voice slows and becomes eerie and low.*

Beach DJ V/O   Daaaas Isssst Paaaaartyyyyyzeeeeiitt.

The lighting also starts to flicker. **Tiny Tim**'s *head appears over the top of the kitchen, the broken sound, lighting and* **Tiny Tim** *all together look very demonic.* **Tiny Tim** *mouth opens and loud static/white noise plays.* **Trevor** *runs in, still tangled in the ghost costume.*

Annie   Oh my God!

Dennis   What's happening!

Trevor   His speaker's knackered, you've got to disconnect him!

Max *climbs up onto Kelly's Dreamhouse and reaches inside* **Tiny Tim**'s *mouth.* **Chris** *flails around choking.* **Tiny Tim** *roars and more lights fall from the rig and smash to the stage.*

Trevor   Mind the lights!

Max   What do I do?

Trevor   Push the red button!

Max   OH MY GOD!!

Max *leans into the mouth to push the button, but falls too far and ends up sliding into the mouth, looking like he's being swallowed whole by* **Tiny Tim**. *The others all scream.*

Robert THE MAN-EATING TROLL! QUICKLY, MARY!

Annie *picks up a stick.*

Annie Run, Santa!

Robert *runs offstage screaming.*

Sandra I said we should have done Cinderella!

Sandra *runs from the stage.* **Annie** *climbs up and drives the stick through* **Tiny Tim's** *head and yanks a handful of cable out of his head. It sinks back down behind Kelly's Dreamhouse and the nightmarish sound and lighting stops.* **Chris** *runs off screaming.*

Annie The man-eating troll is dead!

Sandra God bless us, everyone?

Coins rain down heavily on the cast.

Blackout.

Part IV

Scene 1 – POST SHOW DRINKS

The theatre is empty again. **Sandra** *sits, refreshing her phone.* **Robert** *enters.*

Robert Fingers crossed for a good review.

Sandra Yeah, nothing yet.

Robert I think it went quite well.

Sandra Do you? It ended with a man being swallowed whole by a demented puppet.

Robert You'll be surprised what the audience don't notice. I imagine they didn't even notice I got trapped in that big box.

Sandra Any sign of Chris?

Robert No. Left straight away. Took the Styrofoam goose with him and ran off towards the canal, screaming 'I'm an artist'.

Sandra Right. Did Fleance enjoy it?

Robert He left in the interval, so, maybe.

Jonathan And news on the review?

Jonathan, **Max**, **Annie**, **Trevor** *and* **Dennis** *enter.*

Sandra Nothing yet.

Max (*chuckling*) It's not going to be good.

Annie What am I gonna tell my niece about her Kelly's Dreamhouse?

Robert Ooh! I know how we explain! On Christmas Day I'll climb down the chimney, full costume, and tell her the box got damaged because... it was stepped on by an elf!

Annie Aww. Well she does love Santa.

Robert I could do it as Santa! That's an even better idea.

Annie Do you think Chris is OK?

Sandra Who cares? He deserves what he got.

Jonathan I do feel bad that he heard about the secret meeting.

Dennis Did he? How did that happen?

Robert Maybe I should call him?

Sandra No, don't do that. We're well shot of him.

Trevor Good riddance.

He told me I have the appearance and demeanour of a scotch egg.

Robert *laughs a little.*

Beat.

Dennis So, if Chris is gone, who's our new Prime Minister?

Robert I'll take over. We'll do *Joseph and His Amazing Technicolour Dreamcoat*. But nude.

Sandra No, Robert. Someone else has to be in charge.

Annie Maybe you?

Sandra God no, I don't want to have to deal with all of you.

Robert I am a handful.

Jonathan Well I don't want the job.

Everyone looks at **Annie** *who shakes her head. Everyone then looks at* **Trevor** *who is equally unenthused. The attention then turns to* **Max**.

Max (*laughing*) I'm definitely not leadership material.

Dennis *steps forward.*

All No.

Annie You know, I can't imagine Cornley Drama Society without Chris. It's like fish without chips.

Sandra Like a donut without jam.

Dennis Like a smile without inner pain.

Max (*chuckles*) Is that it then?

Sandra Was that our last ever show?

Robert What a way to bow out.

Chris *has arrived through the door behind them, dripping wet and holding a Tesco's bag. He closes the door and the others turn to see him. Silence.*

Chris Hi.

Annie How you doing Chris?

Chris I'm OK.

Robert Are you sure? You ate your body weight in Styrofoam.

Chris I'm fine.

Sandra Why are you all wet?

Chris I fell in the canal. Fortunately, there was so much Styrofoam in my body I just floated. And as I was in there bobbing around, I realised that perhaps I have made some poor choices. And that I owe you all an apology.

Trevor Are you feeling alright, mate?

Chris I'm better than alright. I feel as light as a feather, as merry as a schoolboy, and as giddy as a drunken man, though that could just be the Styrofoam making its way into my bloodstream. The point is I realised that I need to be better. A better man, a better friend, and if you'll have me a better director. I'm so very sorry.

Annie Look, we're all really sorry too.

Robert We should have all come to you rather than holding secret meetings.

Chris No, Annie. I was so worried about you all ruining my show that I ended up ruining *our* show. Listen, after that man from the council fished me out of the canal I went and –

Chris *opens his bag*.

I know it's not much but I bought a cake. It's the biggest one I could find in the Tesco Express. I thought we could have our first ever after show party.

Chris *hands the cake to* **Trevor**.

Chris If you'll just consider letting me stay I promise from now on things will be different at the Cornley Drama Society. Robert going forward you will play the lead in our next show.

Robert Yes!

Chris Whatever production you like!

Robert The nude -

Chris Not nude.

Robert Well, what's the point then?

Chris Annie, you try so hard to make everyone around you happy and I promise I too will honour Christmas in my heart and try to keep it all the year.

Annie You're speaking weird, Chris.

Chris That is of course if you will have me back?

Robert All in favour.

All raise their hands.

Jonathan It's unanimous. Chris stays on!

All run to **Chris** *for a group hug.* **Chris** *is very uncomfortable.* **Sandra** *breaks the hug suddenly.*

Sandra Wait, what about the review?

Annie Oh who cares about the review? We shouldn't even read it.

Chris Annie's right. What matters is we put on a show. Was it perfect? No. But did it happen? Sort of, yes! We made it almost all the way to the end! And I loved it. Who cares what some reviewer thinks.

Beat. **Sandra** *puts away her phone.*

Sandra You're right. What do the critics know anyway.

Trevor *checks his phone.*

Trevor Review's out.

Sandra Give it to me!

Sandra *takes his phone and scrolls. All jump up and gather round her. 'Oh great!' 'Oooh.' Etc.*

Sandra Culture, regional theatre, here we go. (*Reads.*) At the Cornley Playhouse an amateur production of Christmas Carol was presented.

Beat.

All Wow! Amazing! Yes!

Jonathan That's not negative! There is nothing negative in that review!

Max (*deadly serious*) Well done, everyone. This is excellent news. I am thrilled.

Sandra Wait, there's more. There's more! For all press enquiries contact sandra.wilkinson@msn.com. I got a mention! Yes! I got a mention! I'm coming, Russell! Soon your wife will be dead and it will be me!

Jonathan Hold on, I'll get this up!

Jonathan *goes to the ladder.*

Annie Wait, are you sure?

Jonathan Yeah.

Jonathan *climbs up the ladder and hangs the CONGRATULATIONS banner.*

Sandra Jonathan, you're really high!

Jonathan Oh. Yeah I am, I'm cured! I had nothing to be –

A rung gives way and **Jonathan** *falls backwards.*

Jonathan -AFRAID OOOOFFFFF!!!

Trevor That was the dangerous thing. Alright, shall we take this party down the Dead Duck?

Chris My round!

Robert Thanks, Chris.

Annie Dennis, are you coming?

Dennis What?

Sandra We're all going to the Dead Duck.

Dennis You want me to come?

Chris Of course.

Dennis Thanks. I'd love to!

They all get their coats, bags etc. **Jonathan** *emerges looking dazed.*

Jonathan So what shall we do next?

Chris Oliver?

Robert Yes, Dennis you'd be perfect. You're so thin and malnourished.

Dennis Thank you.

Max Maybe we could do a comedy?

Chris Don't be ridiculous. Comedy is low brow and completely undignified.

They start to leave through the door.

Sandra What about interpretative theatre? I have an idea for a retelling of Romeo and Juliet in which we only use vowels. Oooeeeaoooaaaiii!!!

Robert Oooaaaaiiaaa!!!

Chris No.

Their voices start to fade as they disappear down the corridor.

Annie Come on, Chris! I thought you changed your ways!

The room is left empty with only the **Mr Garibaldi** *puppet alone on his chair. The puppet's head turns to the audience.*

Mr Garibaldi God bless us, everyone!